D1426418

Library of Congress Catalog Card Number 72-102936

Standard Book Number 379-11813-0

# The Middle East:
# Prospects For Peace

*BACKGROUND PAPERS AND PROCEEDINGS*
*of*
*THE THIRTEENTH HAMMARSKJÖLD FORUM*

QUINCY WRIGHT
*Author of the Working Paper*

ISAAC SHAPIRO
*Editor*

Published for
THE ASSOCIATION OF THE BAR OF THE CITY OF NEW YORK

by
OCEANA PUBLICATIONS, INC.
DOBBS FERRY, N. Y.
1969

# THE THIRTEENTH HAMMARSKJÖLD FORUM
## December 4-5, 1968

## Participants

*December 4, 1968*

QUINCY WRIGHT, ESQ.
*Professor, Univ. of Virginia Law School*

ROGER FISHER, ESQ.
*Professor, Harvard Law School*

THE HONORABLE NATHANIEL LORCH
*Member of the Israeli Delegation to the United Nations*

DR. YORAM DINSTEIN
*Israeli Consul in New York*

JOHN J. McCLOY, ESQ.

*December 5, 1968*

HIS EXCELLENCY ABDULLAH EL-ERIAN
*Deputy Permanent Representative
of the U A R to the United Nations*

HIS EXCELLENCY MUHAMMED H. EL-FARRA
*Permanent Representative
of the Kingdom of Jordan to the United Nations*

IRVING M. ENGEL, ESQ.
*Former President, American Jewish Committee*

STEPHEN M. SCHWEBEL, ESQ.
*Director and Executive Vice President,
American Society of International Law*

v

# Table of Contents

PART ONE

THE WORKING PAPER

PART TWO

THE FORUM PROCEEDINGS

Participants: Quincy Wright, Roger Fisher, Nathaniel
Lorch, Yoram Dinstein, John J. McCloy, Abdullah
El-Erian, Muhammed H. El-Farra, Irving M.
Engel, Stephen M. Schwebel

viii

# Editor's Foreword

It is perhaps fair to to say that no human conflict in recent times has presented a greater challenge to the peacemakers than the conflict between Israel and the Arab states, now in its third decade. While the United Nations was instrumental in arranging for the conclusion of armistice agreements after the war of 1948 and in ordering a ceasefire in 1967, it has so far been unsuccessful in its efforts to find a permanent and peaceful resolution of the conflict.

Since the thirteenth Hammarskjöld Forum was held in December 1968, little progress has been visibly made in the pursuit of a peaceful end to the Arab-Israeli conflict. Ambassador Jarring is back at his post in Moscow. The permanent representatives of the United States, United Kingdom, France and the USSR to the United Nations have been meeting almost weekly in an effort (so far unsuccessful) to arrive at a joint proposal of settlement for submission to the parties to the conflict. Meanwhile, ceasefires are not being observed either on the Suez Canal or the Jordan River; Arab commandos continue to commit acts of terror, not only in Israel and the occupied territories, but in areas outside the immediate zone of conflict, such as Greece and Switzerland. Israeli commandos, in turn, have struck, by way of reprisal, not only at targets in Jordan and Egypt but Lebanon as well, even though that country was not a participant in the War of June 1967.

The resolution of the Executive Committee of the Association of the Bar, pursuant to which the Special Committee on the Lawyers Role in the Search for Peace was appointed in 1961, included, among the duties of the special committee, the development of "a program to promote the education of the Bar, and to stimulate discussion among lawyers with respect to the problems of peace." In introducing the first of the Hammarskjöld Forums seven years ago, Lyman Tondel, then Chairman of the Special Committee, said that: "It was felt that the role of law, whatever it might be, should be more fully appreciated, because if there is to be meaningful progress towards peaceful settlement of war and the elimination of war as a means of settling international disputes, then means of settlement alternate to war—means under law—must be developed."

The thirteenth Hammarskjöld Forum was sponsored in the belief that a public discussion of the issues relating to the Arab-Israeli conflict by representatives of the major participants in that conflict as well as by others with special knowledge and views on the subject could contribute to the ultimate peaceful resolution of these issues.

Some years before his death, the late General Douglas MacArthur said that: "War is no longer a feasible arbiter." It is time that the truth of this statement as to the impracticality of military solutions be acknowledged and the Middle East dispute be resolved in a peaceful manner, one which will advance the use of law in the settlement of disputes.

New York, N.Y.
June 1969

ISAAC SHAPIRO,
Member, Special Committee on
the Lawyers Role in the
Search for Peace,
Association of the Bar of
the City of New York

PART ONE

*THE WORKING PAPER*

# The Middle East Crisis

QUINCY WRIGHT

## I. *The Historical Background*

Palestine has been a center of world interest since history began. In ancient times it was the meeting place of Hittite, Egyptian, Assyrian, Babylonian, Persian, Greek and Roman armies, empires, and cultures. With these contacts it is not surprising that it should have given rise to two great religions, Judaism and Christianity, and later have become a major interest of a third, Islam, which converted most of its Arabic population. In the Middle Ages it was the meeting point of Christian and Moslem armies. In modern times, as the holy land of Judaism and Christianity, and second only to the Hedjaz in the reverence of Moslems, it has been the focus of religious interest and pilgrimage, while its position near the Suez canal and the scene of British, Turkish, Arabic and Zionist rivalries has given it political and strategic importance.

The recent history of Palestine has been dominated by the conflict between Arabs and Zionists. Both recognize that the conflict is not racial because both claim to be Semites, nor is it religious because Islam has always tolerated Jews and Christians as "people of the book." Many Jews have lived peacefully in Egypt and other Arabic countries, and 200,000 Arabs have lived peacefully in Israel after its establishment in 1948. The Arabs insist that they have no enmity to Jews but only to political Zionism and the state of Israel which they regard as an imperialistic encroachment on Arab territory. The Zionists, on the other hand say they have no quarrel with Arabs, but only with the Arabic states which refuse to recognize the right of Israel to exist within established frontiers. The conflict, however, has roots in a longer history. It perhaps goes back to the occupation of Palestine by the Jews in biblical times, and

1

their continued quarrels with the Canaanite, Philistine and other inhabitants, whom the Arabs claim as their ancestors.

After the long history of Roman, Byzantine and Turkish occupation of Palestine and of the Jewish diaspora, Arab anxieties were renewed by the Rothschild settlements in the 1880's and the formation of the Zionist organization by Theodor Herzl in 1897 with the object of recovering Palestine as a Jewish state. They manifested much greater anxiety after they became aware of British policy in the area during World War I and especially of the Balfour Declaration of 1917, promoted by the Zionists under the leadership of Dr. Chaim Weizmann who, through his chemical discoveries, had assisted the British war effort.

In 1915, when Turkey entered World War I as an ally of Germany, the Allies, in order to gain Arab support, decided to end Turkish rule in the Arab countries. By the MacMahon agreement of 1915 with Sharif Hussein of Mecca,[1] the British promised to recognize the independence of the Arab states in the Middle East; but by the Sykes-Picot agreement with France[2] in the same year, they promised to recognize a French sphere in Syria and Lebanon along with a British sphere in Iraq and Palestine (including Trans-Jordan) , and by the Balfour Declaration of November 2, 1917,[3] they promised a "national home for the Jewish People" in Palestine.

The Treaty of Versailles included the League of Nations Covenant, which provided in the article dealing with mandates (article 22), that "Certain communities formerly belonging to the Turkish Empire" should be "provisionally recognized (as independent nations) subject to the rendering of administrative advice and assistance by a Mandatory until such time as they are able to stand alone." It further provided that "the wishes of these communities must be a principal consideration in the selection of the Mandatory." Even before peace was finally made with Turkey by the Treaty of Lausanne in 1924, the League of Nations Council confirmed the Middle Eastern Mandates which the Allied powers had assigned in the San

Remo Conference of April, 1920, in accord with the Sykes-Picot agreement, without regard to the wishes of the inhabitants. These wishes had been indicated in the suppressed report of the King-Crane Mission sent to the area by President Wilson during the Paris Peace Conference.[4] The mandate for Palestine was assigned to Great Britain and included the Balfour Declaration.[5]

The Arab countries accepted the British mandate for Palestine without enthusiasm, but during and immediately after the war some Arabs were tolerant of Zionism. On March 3, 1919, Prince Faisal, later king of Iraq, who with T. E. Lawrence had led the revolt in the desert against Turkey during the war, wrote Felix Frankfurter, then a professor at Harvard, later a justice of the U.S. Supreme Court, and an ardent Zionist: "We feel that Arabs and Jews are cousins in race, have suffered similar oppressions...We Arabs, especially the educated among us, look with the deepest sympathy on the Zionist movement. We are working together for a reformed and revived Near East, and our two movements complete one another,... Indeed, I think that neither can be a real success without the other."[6]

The Arabs of Palestine had, it is true, protested against the Balfour Declaration to the King-Crane Commission, had engaged in some rioting against Jewish immigration to Palestine in 1920 and 1921, and had formed a Moslem-Christian Society to defend their rights by petitioning the League of Nations in case of abuses. However, the British pointed out that the Balfour Declaration and the Mandates, while making it a British policy to facilitate the establishment of a national home for the Jewish people in Palestine, were safeguarded by provisions to assure respect for the rights of the Arabs and other non-Jews in Palestine, and of Jews in other countries. These safeguards, insisted on by non-Zionists, were reluctantly accepted by Dr. Weizmann and the Zionists. Doubtless, many Zionists thought that a national home meant a Jewish state. Such a state was certainly the idea of Herzl, but the British white paper of 1922 by Winston Churchill, then Colonial Secretary, made it clear that, in accepting the mandate for Palestine, confirmed by the League of Nations Council, Great Britain intended to establish a cultural home for Jews *in* Palestine, not a Jewish state *of* Palestine.[7] Furthermore, Britain declared in 1922 with approval of the League of Nations Council which supervised the Mandates, that the provisions of the Palestine Mandate providing for the Jewish national home did not apply to Transjordan which was included in that Mandate. This area was given autonomous status under Emir Abdullah, descendent of the Prophet Mohammed, son of King Hussein of Hejaz, brother of King Faisal of Iraq, and grandfather of Hussein who later became king of Jordan. The status of Abdullah was confirmed by a treaty between him and Great Britain in 1928.[8]

With Britain as Mandatory applying the cultural interpretation of the national home and controlling Jewish immigration not be exceed the economic absorptive capacity of the country, the Arabs believed that the principle of self-government stated in the Mandate would eventually be applied. With such application and a population in 1922 of 600,000 Moslems, 73,000 Christians and 84,000 Jews, the Arabs would control Palestine. The Jews were equally certain that the British would not agree to a form of self-government giving the Arab majority a capacity to end Jewish immigration and development of the national home. In fact the British made several proposals for a Palestinian legislative body, but always with the Jewish, plus officially appointed, members constituting a majority as against the elected Arab members, and therefore unacceptable to the Arabs.[9]

When in Palestine in 1925, I discussed the political situation with persons from all parties as well as the government. The British policy was to make Palestine a religious preserve in which the three religions would be assured protection of, and access to, their religious sites. The Jews would be free to maintain a cultural community of moderate size with a high

4

degree of self-government under the ultimate authority of the Mandatory. It was even suggested that eventually the Christians and Moslems would establish similar autonomous cultural homes. There had been considerable Jewish immigration since 1920, bringing the population in 1925 to 835,000 of which 135,000 were Jews and 700,000 Moslem and Christian, mostly Arabs.[10] The British, well aware that a rapid influx of Jews would cause trouble, had controlled immigration, permitting only those with means of support or a trade or profession for which there was a demand to enter the country. This policy maintained order; made it possible to settle disputes peacefully through British courts, the Permanent Court of International Justice, or the League of Nations Council; and promoted a considerable degree of cooperation between Arab and Jewish villages.[11]

Relatively peaceful conditions might have continued indefinitely had it not been for the rise of Hitler, his persecution of Jews, rising international tensions, the unwillingness of most countries to permit Jewish immigration in large numbers, and the consequent pressure for immigration to Palestine. The British occasionally yielded to this pressure, though not enough to satisfy the Zionists and too much to prevent rising tension among the Palestinian Arabs. Jewish immigration increase, especially after Hitler began his persecution of Jews and, as the Jews acquired more land, Arab anxieties increased. Disputes arose over immigration regulations, religious sites (the Wailing Wall, 1929), land ownership, and the position of the Zionist organization in Palestine, leading to a violent Arab revolt in 1936. A British Commission in 1937 (Peel)[12] proposed partition of Palestine between a Jewish state and an Arab area to become part of Trans-Jordan, but this was not implemented because of Arab objections. To placate the Arabs the British modified the criteria for immigration in order to give consideration to political stability as well as economic capacity, and finally in the MacDonald White Paper of 1939,[13] when the Jewish population had reached nearly a third of the entire population of a million and a half, the British declared that it would be maintained at this proportion, with the result that Jewish immigration would be limited to half of the natural increase of the Arab population. The Zionists were dissatisfied and called for partition of the country and a Jewish state.

## II. *The Situation Since World War II*

During World War II, the Zionists and the Jews of Palestine cooperated with the British, but after the war the demand for an independent Jewish state increased, as did Arab-Jewish tension in Palestine. Finally the problem became too much for the British in their weakened position after the war and they placed the problem before the United Nations General Assembly in February 1947, declaring that they would give up the Mandate by August 1, 1948[14] The General Assembly set up a Special Committee on Palestine (UNSCOP) which proposed partition of the country into a Jewish state of Israel and an Arab state, linked by economic institutions for customs union, common currency, and common regulation of irrigation, transport, and communication.[15] A division of revenues to elevate the lower economic level of the Arabs and internationalization of Jerusalem and surrounding territories including most of the holy sites were also proposed. A minority report had recommended a federation but the majority thought this would require more cooperation between Jews and Arabs in Palestine than was available because of radical disagreement on the issue of immigration. The Arabs considered any form of partition illegal under the Charter (article 80) unless they consented, but the General Assembly rejected by one vote a resolution requesting an Advisory Opinion of the International Court of Justice on the question.

The General Assembly then accepted the majority report on November 29, 1947 over Arab protests by a vote of 33 to

13 with ten abstentions and recommended enforcement by the Security Council. Of the Great Powers the United States, France and the Soviet Union voted with the majority, Great Britain and China abstained, and the Arab states declared that they would resist application of the resolution.[16] The Zionists accepted the Partition Plan but the Arabs prepared for armed resistance. Hostilities occurred within Palestine in the winter of 1948. Israel declared its independence on May 14, 1948,[17] and was promptly recognized by the United States, the Soviet Union, and other states. Neighboring Arab states opened hostilities against it, were defeated, and half a million Arabs fled from Israel. Count Folke Bernadotte, president of the Swedish Red Cross, was sent by the United Nations as mediator. He concluded temporary truces but was assassinated in the summer of 1948 by Jewish terrorists. Further hostilities took place in the fall of 1948 and Israel's representative in the United Nations, while insisting in the General Assembly that the territory awarded it by the United Nations resolution of November 29, 1947, was the minimum to which Israel was entitled, declared that, in view of the Arab refusal to accept the award and invasion across the boundary, Israel was free to continue its occupations resulting from the war until such time as a permanent boundary was negotiated, and in any case it would not withdraw from the parts of Jerusalem it had occupied nor accept the internationalization of that city proposed in the United Nations resolution of 1947 and reaffirmed in several resolutions.[18] Ralph Bunche of the United Nations Secretariat, who had succeeded Count Bernadotte as mediator, concluded armistice agreements in 1949 between Israel and each of its Arab neighbors, the last on July 20, 1949,[19] all at approximately the line of the Israeli occupation. These lines embraced fifty per cent more territory than had been accorded to Israel by the United Nations resolution of 1947.[20] The United Nations Truce Supervision Organization (UNTSO), already in existence was continued to supervise the observance of the armistice agreements,[21] and

7

Palestine Conciliation Commission consisting of representatives of France, Turkey and the United States was established to facilitate agreement between Israel and the Arabs especially on the problems of Jerusalem and the refugees. It came near to achieving an agreement at a meeting in Lausanne in 1949 and in 1961 it appointed a special representative, Joseph E. Johnson, President of the Carnegie Endowment for International Peace, to discuss the refugees problem but no agreement was reached.[22]

Egypt considered itself in a state of war with Israel, closed the Suez Canal to Israeli ships and cargoes, and took a leading part in forming the Arab League which included among its aims the elimination of Israel and return of the refugees to an Arab state of Palestine.

Frequent violations of the armistice agreements came before the Security Council during the next years, culminating in a large-scale invasion of the Sinai Peninsula by Israel in 1956 allegedly for the suppression of "Fedayeen" raids, followed by Anglo-French operations against Egypt because of its nationalization of the Suez Canal. An American-proposed resolution, implying that Israel was the aggressor, was vetoed in the Security Council by Great Britain and France.[23] The problem was then turned over to the General Assembly under the Uniting for Peace Resolution of 1950 and, with vigorous support from the United States and the Soviet Union, the General Assembly succeeded in bringing about a cease fire, withdrawal of Israeli, British and French forces to their positions before hostilities, and the establishment of a United Nations Emergency Force (UNEF) in Egyptian territory south of the cease fire line. Israel would not permit the force in its territory. Egypt agreed to the opening of the Straits of Tiran to Israel shipping to its port of Elath on the Gulf of Aqaba.[24] After 1957, breaches of the cease fire line on the Egyptian, Jordanian, and Syrian frontiers continued to come before the Security Council which usually passed a resolution criticizing the excessive Israeli retaliation against minor Arab raids.

The United Nations made continuing efforts to settle the conflict but tensions increased. The Israelis, inspired by a powerful nationalistic sentiment armed for defense, expecting assistance from Zionist, and even non-Zionist Jews outside of Palestine, and importing arms from the United States and other countries. The Arabs, organized in the Arab League, led by President Nasser of the United Arab Republic with headquarters in Cairo, prepared to bring pressure on Israel by economic embargoes, navigation discrimination, diversion of rivers and development of opinion, in and outside the United Nations, sympathetic to the unfortunate situation of the Arab refugees who in 1965 number over one million. Anti-Israel propaganda was continuous and at the Cairo Arab Summit Conference of 1964 an agency was established to maintain the "Arab personality" of Palestine.

Against this background a new crisis arose in 1967, with increased border raids in April, President Nasser's demand on May 16 for withdrawal of the United Nations Emergency Force from Egyptian territory, and his declaration on May 23 closing the Straits of Tiran to Israeli shipping.[25] According to David G. Nes, deputy chief of the American Embassy in Cairo, Nasser took these actions because he had intelligence reports from Syria and the Soviet Union warning of intensive Israeli build-ups on the Syrian frontier. The American Embassy on the basis of its own intelligence reports advised the Egyptian foreign ministry that there was no truth in these reports as, indeed, Nasser later recognized, but Egypt, at the time, believed that the United States was covering up for Israel and proceeded with defensive measures. It strengthened its alliances with Jordan and Syria and moved forces into the Aqaba area, the Israeli frontiers in Sinai, and the Gaza strip, although it declared that it would not attack unless Israel launched an armed attack against its Arab neighbors. According to Mr. Nes, if the United States had paid more attention to Egypt's requests for economic aid during the preceding eleven months and had attempted to demonstrate to Nasser "that we were not hostile" to him, we might have been able to dissuade him from the action which led to war. "Nobody in Washington," he said, "was willing to take the political risk involved in doing anything for Egypt."[26]

President Johnson characterized Nes's view as "parochial,"[27] but on June 19 he expressed a broad view of the situation suggesting that a blocking of the Gulf of Aqaba was illegal and that it was traditional American policy to support the independence and territorial integrity of all Middle Eastern states, that peace in the Middle East required opening the Suez Canal to Israeli shipping, a solution of the refugee problem, and an end of Arab belligerency against Israel.[28]

## III. *The Position of the Belligerents*

Israel claims the rights of a sovereign state within the territory it has occupied within the armistice lines of 1949, because of biblical ascription and historical connection since the time of Moses; effective occupation since 1949; and general recognition by virtue of the Balfour Declaration (1917), the mandate (1921), the United Nations partition resolution (1947), its Declaration of Independence recognized by many states (1948), the armistice agreements (1949), and its admission to membership in the United Nations (1949).[29] In regard to the crisis in 1967 it contended in the United Nations debate that the crisis began in April with increased Arab violations of Israeli territory, Syrian pressure with Egyptian support, and Nasser's defensive alliance with Jordan, manifesting a policy of encirclement of Israel by Egypt, Jordan, and Syria. Mobilizations and movements of forces to the area from Algeria, Iraq, and Kuwait; Nasser's continuous affirmation that a state of war existed with Israel and had existed since 1948; his continued declaration of a policy to restore Palestine to the Arabs and to terminate the existence of Israel—all added to the latter's anxiety. Nasser's demand

10

on May 16 that the United Nations Emergency Force, which had kept moderate peace on the Egyptian frontier since 1957, be withdrawn, Secretary-General U Thant's compliance with this demand on May 18, Nasser's declaration closing the Straits of Tiran and the Gulf of Aqaba to Israeli shipping on May 22, and Nasser's movement of forces into the Aqaba and Sinai areas constituted, in Israel's opinion, clear evidence of aggression. Israel, however, asserted that it withheld its attack on Egyptian forces in Sinai on June 5 until its territory had been attacked on the ground and in the air.[30]

The Arab representatives insisted in the U.N. debate that Arab occupation of Palestine for a thousand years gave them a better historical claim than the brief control by the Israelites two thousand years ago and that their right was recognized by the MacMahon agreement of 1915 and the League of Nations Covenant. In regard to the crisis of 1967 Egypt and other Arab countries claimed that the basic problem was the planting of Zionism in Palestine by Britain to serve colonial interests, and Israel's constant aggressive policy of territorial expansion, together with the expulsion of the indigenous population. Recent provocations had induced the Arab states to cooperate to defend the Arab nation by all measures. The Egyptian request for the removal of UNEF and its closure of the Gulf of Aqaba were said to be within the domestic jurisdiction of Egypt and designed to restore the situation to what it had been before 1956. In any case, they were considered permissible acts in view of the state of war which existed between Israel and the three legitimate littoral states on the Gulf, a situation not affected by the armistice. In fact, the very use of the term "armistice" was said to imply a state of war. Egypt asserted that peace required "a total respect for the Palestine Arab people." It declared, however, that it did not contemplate any offensive action and insisted that it had not taken any such action until attacked by Israel assisted, it said, by the United States and Great Britain, on June 5, 1967.[31]

11

## IV. *United Nations Action*

The United Nations Security Council met on request of Canada and Denmark continuously from May 24 to June 14, 1967, and put the Middle Eastern situation on its agenda over the opposition of the Soviet Union, Bulgarian and Mali delegates. It invited the United Arab Republic (Egypt) and Israel to attend, and later Jordan, Syria, Lebanon, Iraq, Saudi Arabia, Libya, Morocco, Pakistan, and Tunisia.[32] It also discussed the problem on July 8 and 9 and October 25, on request of Israel and the United Arab Republic, to consider violations of the cease fire, and on November 9-22, on request of the U.A.R., to examine principles and procedures for settlement of the conflict.

The General Assembly met in emergency session on June 17, after Israel had declared the annexation of Jordanian Jerusalem, and continued discussion of the situation through July. On July 4 it passed a resolution (99-0-20) declaring Israel's attempt to change the status of Jerusalem was invalid and calling on it to renounce its action.[33] It also passed a resolution on the same day (116-0-2) calling on the parties to observe humanitarian principles and human rights.[34] On July 21 it requested the Secretary-General to report its debates to the Security Council, which should resume consideration of the situation as a matter of urgency.[35]

The discussions in the Security Council indicated wide differences of opinion about responsibility for the crisis and the hostilities. The Soviet Union, Bulgaria, France and Mali, as well as the Arab states, Lebanon, Syria and Jordan, supported the United Arab Republic's position urging that Israel be found guilty of aggression and that no other aspects of the problem be considered until Israel had withdrawn from the territory that it had occupied as the result of the hostilities. India, Nigeria, and Ethiopia agreed on the latter position but the United States, Great Britain, Brazil, Canada, and Denmark thought that a cease fire should be established

12

first without consideration of responsibility for initiation of the crisis and that withdrawal from the occupied territories should be contingent on settlement of other aspects of the conflict. They suggested that restoration of the situation which had led to three instances of serious hostility since 1948 was not a proper solution. They did not, however, support the Israeli contention that the U.A.R. was responsible, nor Israel's suggestion that bilateral negotiations between Israel and each of its Arab neighbors was the only way to establish peace in the area. The United States representative, Arthur Goldberg, supported a suggestion in Secretary-General U Thant's report of May 26, 1967,[36] that the first step was agreement on a "breathing spell to allow tension to subside from its present explosive level." After that, he thought efforts should be made to deal in longer-range terms with detailed points of tension which the Secretary-General had identified in his report.[37]

The Council was unable to pass any resolutions before hostilities broke out on June 5, but passed several after that date providing for and implementing a cease fire,[38] and calling for the protection of civilians in occupied territory.[39] These resolutions were all passed unanimously. During the debate, the Soviet representative intimated that the Socialist countries would take measures to effect the withdrawal of Israeli occupation if the United Nations failed to act.[40] The U.S.S.R. seems to have been somewhat placated by the unanimous passage on November 22 of a resolution[41] introduced by Great Britain providing for the presence of a United Nations mediator in the area to seek conciliation on the basis of principles resembling those stated by President Johnson in an address of June 19, 1967,[42] and recognizing that, eventually, territory occupied by Israel should be evacuated and claims of a state of belligerency by the Arabs terminated.

## V. Legal Issues

Among thirteen legal problems involved in the Middle Eastern situation of 1967, one, (1) the validity of the Balfour

13

Declaration, arose in World War I. Eight arose in the Arab-Israel war of 1948-49; they include (2) the partition of Palestine, (3) the status of Jerusalem, (4) the legality of Arab belligerency, (5) the boundaries of Israel, (6) the use of Jordan waters, (7) the rights of Palestinian refugees, (8) Israel's rights of navigation in the Suez Canal, and (9) freedom of navigation through the Straits of Tiran and in the Gulf of Aqaba. Four additional problems arose in the crisis of 1967: (10) the status of the United Nations Emergency Force, (11) the obligation of Israel to evacuate occupied territory, (12) the responsibilities of the United Nations and the Great Powers, and (13) the responsibility for initiation of the six-day war. This large and unlucky number of problems means that each can be dealt with only briefly.

## A.   *Balfour Declaration*

The Arabs claimed that the Balfour Declaration,[43] which provided a national home for the Jewish people in Palestine, and its incorporation in the British Mandate for Palestine, confirmed by the League of Nations in 1922, constituted an imperialistic *demarche* designed to infiltrate a country which had been Arab for centuries with a European population and to assure British dominance in the area adjacent to the Suez Canal, which would be strategically important to Britain if its occupation and protectorate of Egypt should come to an end. Furthermore, the Arabs claimed that the Declaration was contrary to agreements made with the Arabs to gain their support in the war against Turkey during the First World War. Also, the wishes of the inhabitants were not consulted in awarding the Mandate for Palestine to Great Britain as was required by the League of Nations Covenant. The latter points had been supported by some British representatives in the Middle East, such as Colonel T. E. Lawrence and Miss Gertrude Bell, who believed that the Arabs had been double-crossed.

The motives for the Balfour Declaration appear to have

14

been mixed: gratitude for Jewish support in the war, especially for the chemical experiments of Chaim Weizmann, the head of the Zionist organization, and belief in the legitimacy of the cultural interests of the Jews in Palestine. Strategic consideration for British interests in the Middle East, especially to counteract French interests in Lebanon and Syria, were also involved. The meaning of the MacMahon agreement of 1915[44] has been controversial. The British contend that in promising to support independent Arab states, Palestine was excluded.[45] The Allies, including the United States, recognized the Balfour Declaration and the British Mandate. Furthermore, the Arab leaders accepted them after Transjordan had been excluded from the national home provision and after the Churchill White Paper of 1922[46] had interpreted the meaning of the "national home," not as a Jewish state *of* Palestine but as a cultural community *in* Palestine, and had emphasized the British intention to assure protection for the Arab inhabitants and for the three religions interested in Palestine, as required by both the Balfour Declaration and the Mandate. British policy observed these commitments during the 1920's and the relations between the Arab majority and the Jewish minority were on the whole friendly.[47] However justified the Arab protest against the Balfour Declaration and the British Mandate may have been in 1919, it has been contended that the issue had become moot before 1947 because the legality of the conditions they established had been recognized by most states, including the Arab states, for many years and had been confirmed in the United Nations Charter (article 80).[48]

Only after the large immigration of Jews into Palestine, especially as the result of Hitler's persecutions, was there serious conflict between Jews and Arabs in Palestine and serious anxieties among surrounding states. The Jewish demand for partition and creation of a Jewish state increased Arab alarm and revived objections to the Balfour Declaration.

15

## B.  *Partition of Palestine*

The legality of the General Assembly's recommendation for partition of Palestine was doubtful. Many Zionists had always wanted a Jewish state of Palestine in spite of the acceptance by Chaim Weizmann, Judah Magnes, and other Zionist leaders, of the British concept of a cultural rather than a political Jewish home in Palestine. A Jewish state was, however, increasingly demanded by the Zionists, as the need for a haven from Hitler's persecutions developed in the 1930's, and as the antagonism between Arabs and Jews in Palestine increased with the flood of immigration.

The United Nations Charter provided that mandated territories might be placed under trusteeship (article 77) by agreement of the states directly concerned including the mandatory power (article 79). But the following article added:

> [N]othing in this Chapter shall be construed in or of itself to alter in any manner the rights whatsoever of any states or any peoples or the terms of existing international instruments to which Members of the United Nations may respectively be parties.

The reference to "peoples" in the article seems to have been primarily designed to protect the rights of the Jewish people to a national home in Palestine under the Mandate, but the term also applied to the Arabs in Palestine. The Mandate provided for "safeguarding the civil and religious rights of all the inhabitants of Palestine, irrespective of race and religion" (article 2).

When Britain, despairing of any settlement of the Palestine problem, declared in February 1947 that it would give up the Mandate and withdraw from Palestine by August 1, 1948 (later changed to May 14) and placed the problem before the United Nations General Assembly, the Arabs at once claimed that no change in the Mandate was permissible without the consent of the Arab people of Palestine. The

16

General Assembly's committee, however, recommended the partition of the territory with economic union, and permanent internationalization of Jerusalem and surrounding territory containing most of the religious sites.[49] The Arabs objected and demanded an Advisory Opinion of the International Court of Justice on the compatibility of this action with the Charter (article 80).[50] This demand was rejected by the committee by a vote of 20 to 21 with 13 abstentions.[51] France favored submission to the Court, the United States and the Soviet Union opposed it, and the United Kingdom and China abstained. The General Assembly then accepted the committee's recommendation on November 29, 1947, by a vote of 33 to 13 with 10 abstentions.[52] The United States, the Soviet Union and France voted "aye" and the United Kingdom and China abstained. It was argued that the General Assembly had full power to deal with Palestine because Great Britain, as Mandatory, had under the Mandate (article 1) "full powers of legislation and administration, save as they may be limited by the terms of the mandate" and had transferred these broad powers to the General Assembly, which had succeeded to the League of Nations Council in ultimate sovereignty of mandated territories.[53] Furthermore, article 80 of the Charter, in declaring that the Chapter on Trusteeship could not "in or of itself" alter the rights of "peoples" under the Mandate, did not preclude modifications of these rights by permissible action.[54]

Recognizing that there might be difficulties in implementing its resolution, the General Assembly "requested" the Security Council to "determine, as a threat to the peace, breach of the peace or act of aggression in accordance with article 39 of the Charter, any attempt to alter by force the settlement envisaged by the resolution." The Security Council, however, refused to authorize enforcement measures. The principal proponent of this refusal, the United States Representative (Austin), maintained that the Charter authorized the Council to take such measures only to preserve inter-

17

national peace, not to enforce a political settlement in the mandated territory. He considered the Plan of Partition to be a *recommendation* of the General Assembly.[55]

In view of the terms of the Mandate and the apparent intent of article 80 of the Charter to protect the rights of all the peoples of Palestine, the Palestinian Arabs seem to have had a good legal case, and it is unfortunate that an Advisory Opinion was not obtained on the issue. If the General Assembly's resolution could not be regarded as authoritative, but as a recommendation ignoring its responsibility under article 80 of the Charter, and if Great Britain was unable, as it said it was, to meet its responsibility as Mandatory to protect the rights of the Arab peoples, forcible resistance to partition by the Arabs of Palestine should be regarded as civil strife within the domestic jurisdiction of Palestine in which outside states should not intervene, and in which the United Nations should intervene only if the situation threatened international peace and security.[56] Under this interpretation, however, the Arab states outside of Palestine could justify their intervention in Palestine only by arguing that they were entitled to defend the territorial integrity of Palestine attacked by the Zionists in proclaiming the independence of Israel, and that the Zionists could not justify this declaration by the United Nations partition recommendation which was itself in violation of the rights of the Arab peoples of Palestine under the Charter.[57] In view, however, of the obvious threat to, indeed breach of, international peace, the Security Council should have acted before the Israeli Declaration of Independence, not to enforce partition, but to maintain international peace and security. Its efforts to do so were not effective.[58]

After the defeat of the Arabs in 1948 and the occupation by Israel of large areas of Palestine including parts of Jerusalem, beyond those allotted to it by the General Assembly resolution, the Arab states expressed their willingness to accept, as a basis for peace, the original partition proposal of

18

November 1947 including the internationalization of Jerusalem, to all of which they had at first objected. Israel had at first accepted this proposal but now rejected it, insisting that the territory defined by the armistice belonged to it.[59] In view of the Arab acceptance of the original partition proposal, of the general recognition of Israel as a state, and of its membership in the United Nations since May 1949, it has been contended that an objection to partition as such is not legally valid in 1968.[60]

## C. Jerusalem

Israel's annexation of Jerusalem is difficult to justify on legal grounds. The original Partition Plan of the United Nations provided for the internationalization of Jerusalem and this internationalization was confirmed by an Assembly resolution of December 11, 1948,[61] and again by a resolution of December 9, 1949,[62] which entrusted the administration of the area to the Trusteeship Council. The president of the Council reported to the General Assembly in June 1950 that Israel and Jordan had refused to cooperate in the matter, but the Assembly took no action.[63] Israel continued to occupy portions of Jerusalem outside of the wall included within the armistice line of 1949, made large investments of capital, and established educational and medical institutions in the area, thus providing a *de facto* but not a *de jure* claim. The annexation by Jordan of old Jerusalem east of the 1949 armistice line was equally contrary to the United Nations resolutions but has also established a *de facto* claim. The Arabs at first rejected but later accepted partition as provided in the original United Nations resolution[64] and with exception of Jordan continued to insist on the internationalization of Jerusalem. The United States, the United Kingdom, and the Soviet Union voted against subsequent resolutions in the General Assembly affirming the internationalization of Jerusalem, but these resolutions were approved by a two-thirds majority, partly because the Latin American states voted on

19

this issue with other Catholic states, as desired by the Vatican, rather than with the United States.[65] No state seems to have recognized Israel's annexation of old Jerusalem since June 1967, and the General Assembly twice declared the annexation invalid.[66] In his address to the General Assembly on October 8, 1968, Israeli Ambassador Abba Eban gave no indication of willingness of Israel to withdraw from Jerusalem as called for by these resolutions though Israel "did not," he said, "seek jurisdiction in the holy places of Christianity and Islam."[67]

The status of Jerusalem remains controversial. The interest of the Christian and Moslem communities of the world, as well as that of the Jewish community, for full protection of their holy sites in the area, will have to be satisfied before the issue can be settled.

### D. State of War Alleged by Arabs

The claim of the Arab states that they have been in a "state of war" with Israel since 1948 and that, therefore, they exercise belligerent rights which are not contrary to the terms of the armistices, including closure of the Suez Canal and the Straits of Tiran to Israeli shipping, is probably contrary to the obligation of these states under the United Nations Charter by which both they and Israel are bound.

A state of war in the legal sense, as understood in the 19th century, implied a period of time during which two or more political entities are *equally* entitled to settle a conflict by the use of armed force.[68] It implied a continuing threat by each belligerent during this period to use force against the other, actual use of force when deemed expedient, and impartial neutrality by other states. Nineteenth century international law did not limit the right of a sovereign state to initiate a "state of war" in this sense, although the law of war imposed limitations upon the methods permissible during the war. The Hague Conventions of 1907 imposed minor sub-

20

stantive and procedural limitations upon the initiation of war, and the League of Nations Covenant imposed further restrictions. The Kellogg-Briand Pact of 1929, as interpreted by the Nuremberg Tribunal in 1945, and the United Nations Charter, however, put major limitations upon the use of force in international relations and "outlawed" a legal "state of war" altogether.[69] The members of the United Nations are obliged "to settle their international disputes by peaceful means" and to "refrain in their international relations from the threat or use of force against the territorial integrity or political independence of any state, or in any other manner inconsistent with the purposes of the United Nations."[70]

States may, it is true, use force, in "individual or collective self-defense against armed attack,"[71] or under authority of the United Nations,[72] but in such circumstances the belligerents are not equal; one is in principle the aggressor and the other the defender, and other states may not, according to the Charter, be neutral.[73] A "state of war" is, therefore, "outlawed."[74] Israel, as a state and a member of the United Nations, is recognized under the Charter as the "sovereign equal" of all other members, and the Arab states, as fellow members of the United Nations, cannot under the law of the Charter be in a "state of war" with it. Israel therefore has the right, under the Charter, to demand that the Arab states abandon their claim of belligerence against it and their claim that it has no right to exist.

The Arab states argue that the Zionists were the aggressors in the war of 1947-1949 and in any case the partition was illegal under the Charter and the Arabs were entitled to make war to defend the territorial integrity of Palestine.[75] They also insist that recognition of Israel and its admission to the United Nations violated the rights of the Arab people under the Charter and gave Israel no rights under international law. The armistices they say did not terminate, but

21

only suspended, the existing state of war.[76] These arguments are political rather than legal.

## E. Boundaries

The boundaries of Israel remain undetermined. The old principle that title to territory can be acquired by completed conquest can hardly be supported by the international law of the Kellogg-Briand Pact and the United Nations Charter which forbid war as an instrument of national policy or the use of force against the territorial integrity of any state.[77]

The United Nations Conciliation Commission at the Lausanne meeting on May 12, 1949, reached agreement with Arab and Israeli delegations in regard to territorial adjustments and related refugee rights, but this was later rejected by Israel,[78] and no agreement has since been reached.

Israel has contended that the war of 1949 was initiated by the Arabs, that it was entitled to act in defense, and that the armistice line, after 20 years, constitutes an international boundary. Ceasefire or armistice lines, it is true, establish possessory rights, so long as they remain valid, but they do not in principle establish international boundaries.[79] They may do so in the absence of a boundary treaty or adjudication, by the principles of "prescription" and of "general recognition." The first of these principles would establish the title of the occupant up to the cease fire line if its occupation were not contested by the state adversely affected for a considerable period of time. Fifty years was accepted in the British Guiana-Venezuela arbitration of 1899.[80] The continuous insistence by the Arab states, since the occupation of 1949, that they do not accept the armistice lines as Israeli boundaries, at least beyond the original United Nations resolution of 1947, precludes any Israeli title by "prescription" to the enlarged area of Israeli occupation resulting from the armistices of 1949 or of 1967.

Israel has been "generally recognized" as a state with title to the territory awarded to it by the United Nations resolution of 1947, which the Arab states were prepared to accept as a basis for peace in 1949. There seems to be no such "general recognition" of the additional territory occupied during the hostilities of 1948 or of 1967. Israel's title to occupied territory beyond that of the United Nations resolution of 1947, therefore, remains to be determined by agreement with its neighbors or, perhaps, by "general recognition," manifested by diplomatic acceptance or acquiescence by most states including the Arab states or in a resolution of the United Nations General Assembly.[81]

## F. *Jordan Waters*

The Jordan River has tributaries rising in Syria and Lebanon above the Sea of Galilee, and in Jordan between that Sea and its terminus in the Dead Sea. The lower part of the river was within Jordan's territory before the June war; it now forms the cease fire line between Jordan and the territory occupied by Israel. Proposals by Israel to divert water from the Sea of Galilee to irrigate the Negev, thus depleting the water available for irrigation in Jordan, and proposals by Syria, Lebanon and Jordan to divert or utilize the tributaries of the Jordan in their territories, thus depleting the water available to Israel, have caused continuous controversy and occasional hostilities.[82]

Apart from rights in respect to navigation, international law recognizes the right of all states in a river basin to an equitable share of the river waters for purposes of irrigation, domestic uses, and power; to prohibit diversion or pollution by an upper riparian in violation of equitable claims by lower riparians (on the principle of *sic utere tuum*); and to urge agreement among the riparians to determine equitable shares.[83] No such agreement has been reached among the states of the Jordan basin and the above noted proposals for unilateral diversion by Israel and the Arab states seem to violate the principles of international law on the subject. An international administration with authority, similar to that of the Tennessee Valley Authority in the United States, to maximize the use and to assure equitable distribution of Jordan waters for irrigation, power, and other purposes, has often been advocated, was recommended in the United Nations partition resolution of 1947, and would be beneficial to all the states in the area. Agreement on such an administration is not likely, however, until the political problems have been solved and tension and hostility between Israel and its Arab neighbors have been reduced.

## G.  *Refugees*

The Arab states appear to have a good claim under international law to repatriation or compensation for the Arab refugees from Palestine resulting from the hostilities of 1949 and 1967.[84] It is controversial whether the refugees were compelled by Israel to leave, fled from fear aroused by the Israeli destruction of some villages, or were urged by the Arabs to leave until the Arabs had won the war. The rules of war of humanitarian character designed to protect "human rights" are applicable to all *de facto* hostilities,[85] and require the occupant to spare the civil population. Refusal to allow repatriation or compensation would therefore violate the law of war. Efforts to negotiate a settlement for the million refugees resulting from the war of 1948-49 have been made, especially by the U.N. Conciliation Commission.[86] Israel has made some gestures toward compensation and proposed in the General Assembly on October 8, 1968, a five year plan for refugee integration in the Middle East with acceleration of action for uniting families.[87] These refugees have, in fact, been living for nearly twenty years in Jordanian, Egyptian, and Syrian territory with support from the United Nations and with little effort made by the Arab states to resettle them in other parts of the Arab world, doubtless because the situation is regarded as an asset in keeping world opinion alive to Arab grievances against Israel. Agreement to solve this problem is of great importance from humanitarian, legal, and political

24

points of view. The problem is magnified by more than 350,000 new refugees from the areas occupied by Israel in the six-day war.[88]

Under general international law, a state may protest against, and demand reparation for, injury to its nationals by act or negligence of another state in violation of an obligation under international law. Egypt, Jordan, and Syria may, in accord with this principle, protest to Israel for injuries to their nationals who fled or were expelled from territories which belonged to them before the Israeli occupations of 1949 and 1967. Refugees from territory within Palestine, as a result of the 1949 war, were Palestinian nationals and would not be regarded as nationals of neighboring Arab states, even though the nationality laws of those states may have granted special privileges to "Arabs."[89] These states may, however, properly protest on humanitarian[90] and human rights[91] grounds, and, in so far as the refugees fled or were expelled from Palestine and are not permitted to return to their homes, on the ground that they constitute a burden on the state of refuge.[92] The United Nations has a responsibility for refugees on the general basis of denial of human rights and its support of the Palestinian refugees is an acknowledgment of this responsibility.

## H.  *Suez Canal*

Egypt's closure of the Suez Canal to innocent passage by Israeli shipping since 1949 is probably illegal. Egypt has sought to justify this action on the assertion of a state of war and a duty to protect the Canal. The claim that a "state of war" exists, as noted above in part V.D. seems to be invalid. The Constantinople Convention of 1888,[93] among eight major European states and Turkey, declared that the Canal "shall always be free and open in time of war as in time of peace to every vessel of commerce or of war without distinction of flag" (article 1). This seems to require that the Canal be open to Israeli vessels even if there were a "state of war," but

25

Egypt claims that the further provision in the Convention reserving the "rights and immunities" of the Khedive "not affected by the obligations of the treaty" (article 13) authorized Egypt to take "measures which it might find necessary to take for securing by their own forces the defense of Egypt and the maintenance of public order" (article 10), but such measures" shall not interfere with the free use of the Canal" (article II) . Egypt can properly inspect vessels using the Canal to assure their innocence but cannot prevent innocent passage of vessels protected by the Convention.

The terms of the Convention, therefore, give little support to Egypt's claims, but there is also the question whether Israel, not a party to the Convention, can share in its benefits and whether Egypt as sovereign of the Canal area can close the Canal to Israel under its "inherent right of self-defense against armed attack."[94] The terms of the treaty and practice under it, however, indicate that freedom to use the Canal was intended to apply to all states and that the Egyptian right of defense was limited not only to situation of actual armed attack but also, by the terms of the Covenant to measures which do not "interfere with the free use of the Canal" (article II) . The United Nations Security Council on September 1, 1951, denied Egyptian claim that a state of war or defense necessities justified closing the Canal to Israeli shipping and called upon Egypt to "terminate the restrictions on the passage of international commercial shipping and goods through the Suez Canal wherever bound."[95] On October 13, 1956, the Council reaffirmed this position declaring "there should be free and open transit through the Canal without discrimination overt or covert."[96] President Eisenhower expressed support for this position on February 20, 1957, and said:

> We should not assume that, if Israel withdraws (from the Sharm el Sheikh area on the Straits of Tiran), Egypt will prevent Israel's shipping from using the

Suez Canal or the Gulf of Aqaba. If, unhappily, Egypt does hereafter violate the Armistice Agreement or other international obligations, then they should be dealt with firmly by the society of nations.[97]

Israel's foreign minister said in March 1957 that this statement had weighed heavily in reaching the decision that Israel would withdraw its forces behind the 1949 armistice lines.[98]

On April 24, 1957, Egypt declared that it was "Particularly determined . . . to afford and maintain free and uninterrupted navigation for all nations within the limits of and in accordance with the provisions of the Constantinople Convention of 1888" and agreed to submit to the International Court of Justice any dispute on this issue.[99] Egypt, however, did not permit Israel to use the Canal and Israel has not invoked the jurisdiction of the Court probably because it does not wish to raise the issue of the applicability of the Constantinople Convention to non-signatories.[100] Egypt, however, is probably violating international law in closing the Canal to Israeli shipping.

Israel occupied the east bank of the Canal as a result of the June war but it has refused to cooperate in measures which might lead to clearing the Canal of the vessels sunk during the war until Egypt makes a new pledge to open the Canal to its ships and cargoes.[101]

In December 1967 an agreement was reached through United Nations Ambassador Jarring permitting survey and clearing of the southern part of the Canal to permit fifteen foreign vessels, stranded in the center of the Canal, to get out, but Israel claimed that Egypt began to survey the northern sector of the Canal, contrary to the agreement. Hostilities ensued, as a result of which Egypt suspended the entire operation.[102] Israel insisted that Egyptian compliance or non-compliance with this agreement, the first between the two countries since the armistice, was important because it would indicate Egypt's general readiness to honor future agreements

27

with Israel.[103] The incident indicated the mutual suspicions that have made progress toward opening the Canal or settlement of other problems difficult.

### I. *Gulf of Aqaba and Straits of Tiran*

The legal situation in regard to the Straits of Tiran and the Gulf of Aqaba is similar to that of the Suez Canal, though they differ in that freedom of navigation in the straits is a right of all states under general international law, while canals, being under the sovereignty of the state where they are located, are open to navigation only with consent of that state.[104] Under general international law, and the Convention of 1958 on the territorial sea, which Egypt has not ratified but which appears to be declaratory of general international law, international straits connecting portions of the high seas are open to "innocent passage" by vessels of all states.[105] The high seas include seas like the Baltic and the Black Sea with ports of a number of states, in the absence of agreements by all to make it a *mare clausum*. Egypt, Saudi Arabia, Jordan, and Israel all have ports on the Gulf of Aqaba. The Israeli port of Elath is on the territory within the boundaries of Israel as provided in the United Nations resolution of 1947. It is, therefore, within Israel's jurisdiction and makes the Gulf of Aqaba an international sea. Even if the three Arab states on the Gulf attempted to deny Israel's title to Elath and, by aggreement, attempted to make it a closed sea *(mare clausum)*, it would still be open under the Convention of 1958 which provides for "innocent passage" through straits used for international navigation not only between parts of the high seas but also between the high seas and the territorial sea of a foreign state.

The freedom of the Straits and the Sea of Aqaba was assumed after the hostilities of 1949 and 1956, particularly by the United States, and the withdrawal of Israel from the Sinai area was to some extent contingent on this assumption.[106] Egypt's closure of the Straits in May 1967 appears to have

28

been a violation of the rights of Israel as well as of other states except in so far as Egypt might have occasion to exercise self-defense against armed attack.

## J. *United Nations Emergency Force*

The status of the United Nations Emergency Force, which had kept moderate peace on the Israel-Egyptian frontier for nearly ten years, has been controversial, but elaborate exposition by Secretary-General U Thant on June 26, 1967, of the correspondence between Secretary-General Dag Hammarskjöld and Egypt in 1956 makes it clear that the Force could remain in Egyptian territory only with the latter's permission. Consequently, the Secretary-General was obliged to withdraw it when Egypt so demanded in May 1967.[107] This position was supported by two states which had contingents in UNEF and prepared to withdraw them at Egypt's demand.[108] The refusal of Israel to allow the United Nations Force to operate on its side of the cease fire line in 1956, or in 1967 when the Secretary-General suggested that it be moved across the line from Egypt,[109] also indicates the need for consent of the state where such a force is stationed on the basis of a "recommendation" of the General Assembly.

The Security Council seems to have power to make a "decision" binding on all the members of the United Nations to maintain a force in the territory of a state when it deems such action necessary as a provisional or an enforcement measure to maintain international peace and security.[110] That power was exercised in the Congo in 1960, although the original sending of the force to that country was at the request of the Congo Government.[111] The sending of the United Nations Emergency Force (UNEF) to the Middle East was, however, based on a recommendation by the General Assembly, which has no power to make decisions binding on the members.[112] The problem of the United Nations forces is complicated by the refusal of France, the Soviet Union and other members to consider the cost of such forces as a charge

29

on the regular budget of the United Nations to be apportioned among the members of the General Assembly, although the International Court of Justice held in an Advisory Opinion that it can be so apportioned.[113] This "financial veto" by important countries has, however, made the maintenance of such forces subject to voluntary contributions.

It has been argued that, in view of the danger of hostilities if the force were withdrawn, the Secretary General should have consulted the Security Council before acting.[114] Apart, however, from the legal position, the security of the small U.N. force surrounded by much larger national forces ready to move, and the pending withdrawal of some of its contingents made immediate withdrawal necessary.

### K. *Withdrawal of Israeli Forces*

International law seems to require that Israel eventually withdraw its forces to the armistice lines of 1949 which constituted its *de facto* boundary before the six-day war. A state is not permitted to maintain armed forces in the territory of a foreign state without its consent, unless authorized by United Nations decision or required by defensive necessity. The doctrine asserted by Secretary of State Stimson in refusing to recognize any change of rights from the Japanese occupation of Manchuria in 1931 in violation of its obligations under the Kellogg-Briand Pact was accepted by the League of Nations, which held that the occupation also violated Japan's obligation under article 10 of the Covenant.[115] The concept of "no fruits of aggression" implying a duty to withdraw forces from illegally occupied territory has been generally accepted.

Article 51 of the United Nations Charter goes further. It recognizes the inherent right of individual or collective self-defense, in the event of an armed attack, only "until the Security Council has taken measures necessary to maintain international peace and security." This implies that an oc-

30

cupation of foreign territory, even if justified as a defensive necessity, must be withdrawn when peace and security have been restored. Consequently, in the Suez incident of 1956, the United Nations insisted, without deciding who was the aggressor, that the forces of Israel, France and the United Kingdom in Egyptian territory must be withdrawn under the cease fire as the first step in establishing peace.[116] This was affirmed by the unanimously passed Security Council resolution of November 22, 1967 in "emphasizing the inadmissibility of the acquisition of territory by war."

After the Security Council had adopted cease fire resolutions in the six-day war, the Soviet Union, supported by France, the Arab states, India and others, demanded on June 6, 1967, that Israel withdraw from occupied territories. Israel, however, supported by the United States and others insisted that such a withdrawal be accompanied by Arab renunciation of belligerency and perhaps of other policies inconsistent with international law such as exclusion of Israeli shipping through the Suez Canal and the Straits of Tiran.[117] It has not declared its willingness to withdraw from all the territories it occupied in 1967.

While it is true that the Arab states would be hampered in negotiations as long as Israel occupied portions of their territory, and Israel might feel a defensive necessity to continue occupation of certain areas so long as the neighboring Arab states maintain a posture of belligerency, it would seem that both sides should be ready to renounce policies in violation of international law contemporaneously. Return to the situation which has led to three Middle Eastern wars would not seem expedient. A package in which all agreed, not only to accept their obligations under international law and the United Nations Charter, but also to act in accordance with these obligations, would seem an essential condition of peace, as was recognized by the Security Council resolution of November 22, 1967.

The responsibility of the United Nations under the Charter is clear. It should, as it has, demand a cease fire as a provisional measure[118] and, if hostilities cease as a result, it should seek to restore international peace and security by achieving agreement among the parties. Neither the Security Council nor the General Assembly has power to make a binding decision settling the dispute, but either can make recommendations for settlement if the dispute or situation is one "the continuance of which is likely to endanger the maintenance of international peace and security," as the Middle Eastern situation certainly is.[119] Either can request Advisory Opinions from the International Court of Justice to determine legal obligations involved[120] and can recommend that the parties submit legal issues to the Court for binding judgment.[121] The Security Council may decide upon measures to enforce such a judgment.[122]

The United Nations has ordinarily made a return to prewar boundaries part of a cease fire demand.[123] The Soviet Union, the Arab countries, and others believe that its failure to do so in the present instance constitutes a failure to meet its responsibilities.

These states also consider that the United Nations has a responsibility to determine the aggressor in the hostilities.[124] Such a determination, however, has usually been avoided because it is thought that it might complicate the problem of restoring peace. Provisional cease fire measures are addressed to all belligerents and only if one or both parties refuse to accept a cease fire, or after accepting, violate its terms, does the Charter, and practice under it, normally require a determination of the aggressor.[125]

The fact that both Israel and the Arab states had failed to observe obligations under the Charter and international law gave a certain justification for the failure of the United Nations to demand immediate withdrawal of Israeli forces behind the cease fire lines of 1949, although it has been recognized that "to conform to substantial justice the armistice should be proposed before the fighting has resulted in any substantial change in the *de facto* line of occupation and should be based on that line."[126]

Israel has suggested that the great powers, especially the United States, which had facilitated Israel's withdrawal of forces from the Aqaba area in 1957 by assuming that Egypt would open the Suez Canal and the Gulf of Aqaba to free navigation for all states including Israel, had a responsibility to take action when Nasser closed the Straits of Tiran in May 1967.[127] President Eisenhower's statement of February 1957 suggested, however, a general interest in assuring Egypt's observance of its international obligations, rather than a specific commitment made by the United States to induce Israel to withdraw its forces. Such a commitment, beneficial to Israel, would have been contrary to the principle of "no fruits of aggression," which the United Nations was insisting on at that time. Perhaps because of its involvement in Vietnam, the United States took no action in the 1967 crisis beyond a declaration of principle, and the Security Council proved unable to act because some of the great powers favored Israel and others favored Egypt. Prompt action to open the Gulf to Israeli shipping might have prevented the war.

## M. *Determination of Aggression*

Inasmuch as a cease fire was obtained, it was unnecessary and probably undesirable for the United Nations to determine the aggressor in the hostilities and such a determination presented serious difficulties of fact and law.[128] Israel claimed that Egypt's act in closing the Straits of Tiran was a blockade which constituted an act of war against Israel.[129] Egypt's expulsion of the United Nations Emergency Force, and its mobilization of its own forces in the Sinai area and the Gaza strip on the Israeli frontier, was said further to indicate its aggressive intentions. Israel thus claimed that it was the

33

victim of "armed attack" in the broad sense, and was free to act defensively under article 51 of the Charter. It, however, refused to permit UNEF to cross the armistice line to its territory. It claimed at first that it did not actually use armed force against Egypt until the latter had initiated action against it on the ground and in the air, and that defense against Egypt's blockade and the Arab effort to conquer Israel were its sole goals in using force.[130] It later admitted, in effect, that its air attack preceded Egyptian attack on its territory but claimed that Egypt's aggressive acts justified its attack as necessary defense.[131]

Egypt considered that the closing of the Straits of Tiran and the expulsion of UNEF were within its domestic jurisdiction; that mobilization was necessary for defense against Israeli mobilization on the Syrian frontier, of which it allegedly had intelligence reports; that it had no intention of initiating hostilities, and that it did not in fact take military action until Israeli air forces had bombed Egyptian airports, which was followed by simultaneous Israeli action in the Gaza strip, Sinai, Sharm el Sheikh and other areas. "[T]he dimensions of the Israeli attack are so wide," the Egyptian representative in the Security Council said, "that no one can doubt the premeditated nature of this aggression."[132]

Clear evidence of the facts would be important to determine the aggressor, but it would appear that the well-authenticated acts of Egypt, especially its insistence that a "state of war" existed and its policy to terminate the existence of Israel, accompanied by the closure of the Straits of Tiran and extensive mobilization on the Israeli frontier, could be regarded as amounting to an "armed attack" on Israel. On the other hand, Israel's refusal to permit UNEF to cross the armistice line into its territory, its superior military preparations, its continued occupation of Arab territory, and its annexation of old Jerusalem, suggest that Israel had intentions other than defense. Furthermore, its massive air and land attack initiated the war on June 5. The issue of which was the aggressor may not have to be decided in the process of restoring peace, but it may arise in subsequent controversies concerning reparation for injuries received during the hostilities, on the principle that the aggressor should be liable to compensate his victims for injuries resulting from his act of aggression.[133]

Reviewing the thirteen legal issues discussed, it appears to the writer that Israel was in the wrong on three: the annexation of Jerusalem, the continued occupation of Arab territory, and the failure to repatriate or compensate Arab refugees. Arab states were in the wrong also on three issues: the assertion of a state of war with Israel and refusal to recognize the latter's right to exist, the closure of the Suez Canal, and the closure of the Gulf of Aqaba to Israeli shipping. The Arab claims that the Balfour Declaration and the partition of Palestine violated their rights were probably originally valid, but became moot after the general recognition of Israel and its admission to the United Nations. The issue concerning the status of UNEF also became moot after its withdrawal, which seems to have been legally necessary. The responsibility of the United Nations and the Great Powers to insist that the Suez Canal and the Straits of Tiran be kept open continues, as does the responsibility of the United Nations to restore international peace and security. On two issues, those concerning the use of Jordan waters and determination of the boundaries of Israel, both the Arabs and Israelis have manifested imperfect respect for international law and for the necessity to reach agreement. On the issue of responsibility for initiating the six-day war, Egypt made threats and took hostile measures instigating the war, but Israel's large-scale attack on June 5 started the war. Both may be guilty of aggression.

## VI. *Prospects of the Future*

Little progress toward a settlement of the situation had been made by December 1968 apart from establishing cease fire lines. The Security Council after its cease fire of June had been accepted, recognized by unanimous resolution on November 22, 1967 principles of settlement including withdrawal of Israeli forces from occupied territories and Arab renunciation of belligerency, as well as freedom of navigation in the waterways, just settlement of the refugees problem and guarantee of the territorial inviolability and political independence of every state in the area. It also provided for United Nations presence in the area for purposes of conciliation. Ambassador Gunnar Jarring has been seeking a basis for conciliatory action since December 1967. The General Assembly has declared that Israel should renounce its annexation of Jordanian Jerusalem.

Egypt has accepted the Security Council resolution of November 1967 and has negotiated with Ambassador Gunnar Jarring to implement it.[134] Apparently Jordan has done the same, but I have not found clear evidence of the position of Syria and other Arab states on the question.

Israel seems not to have accepted the November resolution and has insisted on direct negotiations with each of its Arab neighbors, rather than negotiations with the United Nations mediator. A statement by Israeli Ambassador Abba Eban to Ambassador Gunnar Jarring on October 4, 1968,[135] and in the General Assembly on October 8 suggests some relaxation of this position. Israel has, however, declared the annexation of old Jerusalem and Israeli Defense Minister Dayan has declared that Israel must retain certain occupied territories. The November resolution called for "withdrawal of Israeli forces in territories occupied in the recent conflict" without specifying whether this meant *all* such territories as demanded by the Arabs.

The military confrontation continues. The Arabs have strengthened their military position by importing Soviet arms and benefitted by the presence of Soviet naval forces in the eastern Mediterranean. Israel has maintained its military preparations and hopes for the support of the United States

36

which also has naval forces in the eastern Mediterranean. The United States, however, has sought to maintain an impartial position by urging settlement of the refugee problem and asserting that Israeli withdrawal from occupied territories must be contingent on Egyptian renunciation of belligerence, recognition of Israel, and opening of the waterways. It also has sought to maintain the military balance of power by giving arms to both Israel and Jordan.

Sporadic hostilities have occurred on the Syrian, Jordanian and Suez frontiers in violation of the cease fire agreements, as well as by Arab guerrillas from inside the occupied territories. The Suez Canal continues blocked and another round of major hostilities between Israel and the Arabs, which might escalate into general war, seems likely unless effective international action, preferably through the United Nations, breaks the deadlock.

It has been suggested that termination of Vietnam hostilities might induce the Soviet Union and the United States to exert influence in common toward realization of the package deal contemplated by the Security Council resolution of November 22, 1967. Both of the superpowers seem anxious to continue their *detente*, which has been hampered by the Vietnam and Czechoslovak interventions, and to establish peace in the Middle East. The ambivalence of their Middle Eastern policies in the past is notable. Both accepted the Balfour Declaration and the British Mandate for Palestine, and the Soviet Union promptly followed the United States in recognition of Israel in May 1948. They were together in supporting the United Nations cease fire in 1956, and in insisting upon withdrawal of the British and French forces, and the evacuation by Israel of the territories it had occupied, as the first step toward settlement of the Suez problem.

However, after the United States had affronted Arab opinion by the Eisenhower doctrine of 1957,[136] thought by the Arabs to manifest United States support of imperialism and Zionism, the Soviet Union has manifested a pro-Arab

37

position, particularly after Communist-oriented parties had developed, especially in Syria and Iraq.

The United States has usually sought to be impartial in the Middle Eastern controversies. It has been anxious to maintain friendly relations with the Arabs because of the interest of American corporations in Middle Eastern oil and a general interest in peace, but domestic politics have urged a pro-Israel policy because of the extensive Zionist influence in such critical areas as New York City. Furthermore, the cold war obsession of Americans has induced the Government to oppose the Soviet Union and Middle Eastern states which accept Soviet aid. After the Soviet Union had given financial and technical support to Egypt to build the Aswan Dam, following United States repudiation of its offer to give such support in June 1956, United States antagonism to Egypt increased.[137]

The positions of Great Britain and France have also been ambivalent. Great Britain has favored the Jewish national home in Palestine, developed it as Mandatory Power for nearly thirty years, and was responsible for placing the serious situation which had developed in 1947 before the United Nations for solution. This resulted in partition of Palestine as desired by the Zionists at that time. Great Britain was also responsible for intervention in Egypt following Israel's invasion in 1956. It has, however, supported the Arab League and the independence of Arab states.

France was allied with Israel and Britain against Egypt in the intervention of 1956 and had followed a pro-Israeli policy until the recent crisis during which it has tended to support the Arab position.

The position of the Great Powers, therefore, seems somewhat flexible and elements in the situation of both Israel and the Arabs militate against excessive rigidity. Arab nationalism, especially Egyptian nationalism, urges avoidance of excessive dependence upon the Soviet Union for arms, and experience in the three wars with Israel suggests caution in getting into another. Some Arab countries such as Tunisia and to a lesser degree Jordan have urged accommodation with Israel.

Israel had a population, within the 1949 armistice lines, which included a majority of oriental Jews most of whom speak Arabic, who feel discriminated against by the government, controlled by European and American Jews, and who, with the two hundred thousand resident Arabs, have favored accommodation with Arab neighbors.[138] It, therefore, would face a serious domestic problem if it attempted to assimilate the recently occupied areas with more than half a million Arabs. If these areas were retained with their present inhabitants, apart from the issue of legality, the western Jews now in control would be a minority of the population of Israel especially if, as has been suggested, the refugee problem were liquidated by settling all the refugees in these areas. If these areas were accorded a semi-colonial status, Israel would jeopardize its claim to be a democracy unless a true federation of the Arab area with Jewish Israel could be effected. If the present population of the recently occupied areas were deported or driven out, the refugee problem would be accentuated and world opinion would be shocked. Annexation of Jerusalem was shocking to Christian and Moslem opinion as indicated by the large majority in the General Assembly opposing it. It seems doubtful whether the strategic advantages of holding the recently occupied territories can compensate for the internal and external difficulties Israel would encounter.

The suggestion that Jews abroad should not be admitted to Zionist organizations unless they promise to migrate to Israel within five years would not only militate against favorable support for Israel among American Jews, who do not usually wish to migrate, but suggests an effort to maintain a majority of westernized Jews to neutralize the influence of the oriental Jews[139] and the Arabs in Israel, perhaps to fill the recently occupied areas if their inhabitants are expelled.

39

Both the Jews and the Arabs would undoubtedly benefit by reaching an accommodation and establishing peace in the Middle East. The Soviet Union, the United States and the world would all profit by eliminating the escalating possibilities of Middle Eastern hostilities. The Security Council's unanimous recommendation, on November 22, 1967, of a settlement, based on mutual recognition of the legal rights of both Israel and the Arabs, indicates a first step. A further step has been suggested by the leaders of the oriental Jewish community in Israel. They have proposed establishment of an "autonomous Palestinian Arab Entity in the occupied area in which all the refugees would be settled."[140] Many of the refugees of 1948 and 1949 are already there. A federation of Israel with such a Palestinian Arab state and perhaps with Jordan was proposed but considered impracticable in 1947. Political independence of these states with economic union was, however, recommended by the United Nations and accepted by the Zionists in 1947 and, after military defeat in 1949, by the Arabs. Return to this proposal, repudiated by the victorious Zionists in 1949, might be considered.[141]

# Notes

1 CMD. No. 5957 (1939).

2 See DOCUMENTS ON BRITISH FOREIGN POLICY 1919-1939, 1st Ser., vol. IV, at 241-51 (E. Woodward & R. Butler, eds. 1952).

3 The text is officially quoted in CMD. No. 5479, at 22 (1937).

4 [1919] 12 FOREIGN REL. U.S. 745, 772-73 (1947).

5 For text of the Palestine Mandate, see, *e.g.*, CMD. No. 1785 (1923) and Quincy Wright, MANDATES UNDER THE LEAGUE OF NATIONS (University of Chicago Press, 1930) , p. 600 ff.

6 Quoted by Count Carlo Sforza, *The Near East in World Politics*, in Ireland, ed., THE NEAR EAST, PROBLEMS AND PROSPECTS (University of Chicago Press, 1942) p. 21. See also Salo W. Baron, *"Prospects of Peace in Palestine," Ibid.*, p. 108; Charles K. Webster, *"British Policy in the Near East," Ibid.*, p. 160.

7 Herbert Samuel, REPORT OF THE HIGH COMMISSIONER ON THE ADMINISTRATION OF PALESTINE, 1920-25 (London, Colonial Office, 1925), p. 24.

8 *Loc. cit.* and Q. Wright, *op. cit.* note 5, p. 205, 409, and text of Mandate (art. 25) and Declaration of 1922, *id.* p. 605.

9 Q. Wright, *The Palestine Problem*, 40 POL. SCI. QUAR., 1926, 389 ff. For population figures see Wright, *op. cit.* note 5, p. 630.

10 This is the average for the decade. Both Arab and Jewish populations increased, the latter at a more rapid rate by immigration of some 10,000 a year. The Jews constituted about 10% of a total population of 800,000 in 1920, 19% of a total population of 1,000,000 in 1930, and 30% of a total population of 1,530,000 in 1940. 17 ENCYCLOPEDIA BRITANNICA 134 (1965). STATEMENT OF BRITISH FOREIGN POLICY (CHURCHILL MEMORANDUM) ON PALESTINE, CMD. No. 1700 (1922) : See Wright, *The Palestine Problem, supra,* for conditions in 1925.

11 *Ibid., The Palestine Problem,* p. 405 ff.

12 CMD. No. 5479 (1937).

13 CMD. No. 6019 (1939).

14 U.N. GAOR (1st Spec. Sess.) 183, U.N. Doc. 286 (1947).

15 G. A. Res. 181, 2 *id.*, Resolutions 131, 132 (1947).

16 *Id.*, Supp. II, U.N. Doc. 364 and Adds. 1-4.

17 FUNDAMENTAL LAWS OF THE STATE OF ISRAEL 8 (J. Badi ed. 1961) ; N.Y. Times, May 15, 1948, at 2, col. 3.

18 3 U.N. GAOR, Pt. I, 1st Comm. 640-43, 644-45, 832, 840-42 (1948). As to subsequent resolutions on Jerusalem see notes 61 and 62 *infra* and accompanying text.

19 Armtice agreements are cited in Elaraby, *Some Legal Implications of the* 1947 *Partition Resolution and the* 1949 *Armistice Agreement*, 33 LAW AND CONTEMP. PROB., p. 104, notes 19-22 (1968) .

20 Maps of the boundaries proposed by the United Nations Plan of Partition with Economic Union and the Armistice agreements are included in N. LORCH, THE EDGE OF THE SWORD: ISRAEL'S WAR OF INDEPENDENCE 1947-1948, at 27 (1961).

21 S.C. Res. 73 (1949).

22 Note 59 infra; EVERYMAN'S UNITED NATIONS, 1945-1963 (7th ed., UN.

41

1964) p. 72-75. The 8th edition (U.N. 1968) p. 94-95, is less complete on the work of the Palestine Conciliation Commission.

[23] 11 U.N. SCOR, 749th meeting 31 (1956).

[24] Developments of 1956-1957 summarized in EVERYMAN'S UNITED NATIONS, cit. note 22 above. See Q. Wright, *Interventions, 1956*, 51 A.M. J. INT'L L., 257 ff., (April, 1957).

[25] See, *e.g.*, reports by Secretary-General to the Security Council, U.N. Docs. S/7896, May 19, 1967, and S/7906, May 26, 1967.

[26] N.Y. Times, Feb. 9, 1968, at 3, col. 4. See also notes 129, 136, 137 *infra*.

[27] *Id.*

[28] 57 DEP'T STATE BULL. 31, 33-34 (1967).

[29] Theodore F. Bousky, *The Claims of the Arab and the Jew to Palestine*, 45 PAPERS OF THE MICHIGAN ACADEMY OF ARTS AND SCIENCES, 265 ff. (1960).

[30] U.N. Docs. S/PV. 1342, May 24, 1967, at 41-45; S/PV. 1343, May 29, 1967, at 62-72; S/PV. 1348, June 6, 1967, at 71-91. Israel later in effect admitted that its air forces had invaded Egyptian territory before the Egyptian attack. See note 131 *infra*.

[31] U.N. Docs. S/PV. 1343, May 29, 1967, at 21-47 (UAR); S/PV. 1344, May 20, 1968, at 17-46 (Syria); S/PV. 1345, May 31, 1968, at 27-50 (Jordan). In an interview in March 1968, Nasser said that his charge that Israel was assisted by the United States was due to a misunderstanding based on suspicion and faulty information. Attwood, *Nasser Talks*, LOOK, March 19, 1968, at 63; N.Y. Times, March 5, 1968, at I, col. 3.

[32] For record of the proceedings see U.N. Docs. S/PV. 1341-1361, May 24-June 14, 1967. Summaries in 21 INT'L ORG. 837-861 (1967); 4 U.N. MONTHLY CHRON., No. 6, at 5-26, and No. 7, at 4-32 (1967).

[33] G.A. Res. 2253, (5th Emer. Spec. Sess.) GAOR Supp. 1, at 4, U.N. Doc. A/6798 (1967), reaffirmed (99-0-18) on July 14, 1967 by G. A. Res. 2254, *id.* at 4.

[34] G.A. Res. 2253, *id.* at 3, summarized, 22 INT. ORG., 567 (Spring 1968).

[35] G.A. Res. 2256, *id.* at 4.

[36] See note 25 *supra*.

[37] U.N. Doc. S/PV. 1343, May 29, 1967, at 7-21.

[38] S.C. Res. 233 (1967); S.C. Res. 234 (1967); S.C. Res. 235 (1967); S.C. Res. 236 (1967).

[39] S.C. Res. 237 (1967).

[40] U.N. Doc. S/PV. 1353, June 9, 1967, at 27-31.

[41] S.C. Res. 242 (1967). See Appendix.

[42] See note 28 *supra*.

[43] See note 3 *supra*.

[44] See note 1 *supra*.

[45] See, *e.g.*, C. SYKES, CROSSROADS TO ISRAEL 63-65 (1965).

[46] See note 6 and 9 *supra*.

[47] Wright, *supra* note 9.

[48] All systems of law provide means such as prescription, general recognition, statutes of limitation, agreements by the interested parties, and legislation, by which situations which originated in illegality become moot or acquire a legal status. The principle *jux ex injuria non oritur* (rights do not arise from wrongs) must be balanced by the principle *ex factis jus oritur* (rights arise from facts), especially in the society of nations which is often unable to rectify wrongs and is faced by a general interest that disputes be terminated. See H. LAUTERPACHT, RECOGNITION IN INTERNATIONAL LAW 427 (1947); Wright, *Recognition, In-*

*tervention, and Ideologies,* 7 INDIAN Y. B. INT'L AFF. 89, 95 (1958). This "principle of effectiveness" must, however, as stated by Verdross, be applied "within the framework of international law" or it "would legalize any illegality and thus abolish international law itself," quoted by KUNZ, THE CHANGING LAW OF NATIONS (Ohio State University Press, 1968), p. 383.

49 See text accompanying note 16 *supra.*

50 2 U.N. GAOR, Ad Hoc Comm. on the Palestinian Question 299-301, U.N. Doc. A/AC. 14/32 (1947).

51 *Id.* at 203.

52 2 U.N. GAOR 1424-425 (1947).

53 T. LIE, IN THE CAUSE OF PEACE 167 (1954); Q. WRIGHT, MANDATES UNDER THE LEAGUE OF NATIONS 528-30 (1930). On the question of sovereignty of mandated territories, see more generally *id.* at 313-537.

54 See also on the partition of Palestine, EVERYMAN'S UNITED NATIONS, *supra* note 24, at 70-71; Wright, note 24 *supra* at 264-266.

55 3 U.N. SCOR 253d meeting 265-67 (1948).

56 In accordance with articles 2(7) and 39 of the Charter since Palestine had been provisionally recognized as a state by the League Covenant (art. 22) and the Mandate. See Wright, *International Law and Civil Strife,* 1959 PROCEEDINGS, AM. SOC'Y INT'L L. 145, 149-51; *The Legality of Intervention Under the United Nations Charter,* 1957 *id.* at 79, 83-85; *United States Intervention in the Lebanon,* 53 AM. J. INT'L L. 112, 119-25 (1959); *Legal Aspects of the Vietnam Situation,* 60 *id.* at 750, 754-55 (1966).

57 On May 15, 1948, the Arab states declared that they "were compelled to intervene for the sole purpose of restoring peace and security and establishing law and order in Palestine" because "peace and order have been completely upset" there constituting "a serious and direct threat to peace and security within the territories of the Arab states themselves." Furthermore, "the security of Palestine is a sacred trust for them," "the spread of disorder and lawlessness to neighboring Arab lands" must be prevented, and "the vacuum created by the termination of the mandate and the failure to replace it by any legally constituted authority" must be filled. 3 U.N. SCOR, Supp. May 1948, at 83, 87, U.N. Doc. S/745 (1948). See also Nabel Elaraby, First Secretary U.A.R. Mission to the U.N., *Some Legal Implications of the 1947 Partition Resolution and the 1949 Armistice Agreements,* 33 LAW AND CONTEMP. PROB., 97, 103 (1968).

58 S.C. Res. 46 of April 17, 1948, affirmed the responsibility of the United Kingdom, so long as it was the Mandatory Power, to maintain peace and order in Palestine, but called on the Arabs and Jews to cease all acts of a military or paramilitary nature, all acts of violence or terrorism, and all importation of arms or armed bands, and to cooperate with the Mandatory Power. S.C. Res. 48 of April 23, 1948, established a Truce Commission and the General Assembly on May 14, 1948 authorized the appointment of a mediator to promote peaceful adjustment of the Palestine situation, and to cooperate with the Truce Commission. U.N. GAOR, 2d Spec. Sess., Supp. 2, Resolutions, at 5 (1948).

59 The Arab states and Israel accepted, at Lausanne of May 12, 1949, a proposal of the U.N. Palestine Conciliation Commission which had been established by G.A. Res. 194 of December 11, 1948 (3 U.N. GAOR, Resolutions 21, 22, U.N. Doc. A/810), and composed of representatives of France, Turkey, and the United States. The proposal provided for a territorial settlement substantially in accord with the Plan of Partition with Economic Union. Third Progress Report of the Palestine Conciliation Commission, 4 U.N. GAOR, Ad Hoc Pol. Comm., Annex, vol. II, at 5, 8-9, U. N. Doc. A/927 (1949). A few days later Israel made territorial proposals which the Arab delegations considered to be in flagrant violation of the Protocol. On September 12, 1949, the Commission expressed the opinion that proposals of both sides exceeded the terms of the Protocol. See General Progress

Report...of the U.N. Conciliation Commission for Palestine..., 5 U.N. GAOR, Supp. 18, at 3-4, 19-21, U.N. Doc. A/1367/Rev. I (1950).

60 See note 48 *supra.*

61 G.A. Res. 194, 3 U.N. GAOR, Resolutions 21, 23, U.N. Doc. A/810 (1948).

62 G.A. Res. 303, 4 *id.*, Resolutions 25, U.N. Doc. A/1251 (1949).

63 Special Report of Trusteeship Council, 5 *id.*, Supp. 9, at I, U.N. Doc. A/1286 (1950); *id.*, Plenary 684 (1950).

64 See note 59 *supra.*

65 See, *e.g.*, vote of December 9, 1949, 4 U.N. GAOR 607 (1949).

66 Note 33 *supra.*

67 22 INT. ORG., 566, 568 (1968) and Abba Eban, *Forward to Peace*, Embassy of Israel, Washington, D.C. (1968). Elihu Lauterpacht seeks to defend Israel's permanent administration of the old city of Jerusalem by insisting that Jordan's occupation of this and other areas of Palestine since 1949 gave it no claim to sovereignty but that Israel could permanently administer the territory after it had occupied it and Jordan had withdrawn because there was a "vacuum of sovereignty" in Palestine outside of Israel after termination of the Mandate. He points out that Israel had not "annexed" the old city, as it had the new city of Jerusalem, but accepted the "functional internationalization" of the holy places distinct from "territorial internationalization" proposed by the U.N. partition resolution and demanded by the General Assembly. Israel had never accepted the latter. *Jerusalem and the Holy Places*, Anglo-Israel Association, London, Pamphlet No. 19, 1967, p. 41 ff. This argument denies the provisional independence of Palestine, recognized by the Covenant (art. 22, par. 4), the Mandate (preamble) and the Charter (art. 80) and its claim to the territory established by the Mandate (art. 25) except in so far as portions may have been generally recognized as within the territory of Jordan or Israel. It also gives military occupations by Israel a status superior to that of Arab occupations. These hypotheses are not likely to be accepted by the Arab states or the United Nations.

68 Q. WRIGHT, A STUDY OF WAR 8, 685, 698 (1942). See also Wright, *Changes in the Conception of War*, 18 AM. J. INT'L. L. 755, 761-67 (1926). F. GROB, THE RELATIVITY OF WAR AND PEACE: A STUDY IN LAW, HISTORY, AND POLITICS (1949) presents numerous instances in which force was used in international relations in various quantities and under various names including "war." He does not distinguish the factual from the legal conception of war and suggests that the latter conception is so lacking in clarity that it is useless.

69 Q. WRIGHT, A STUDY OF WAR 891-92 (1942); *The Meaning of the Pact of Paris*, 27 AM. J. INT'L L. 39 (1933); *The Law of the Nuremberg Trial*, 41 *id.* 38 (1947); *The Outlawry of War and the Law of War*, 47 *id.* 365 (1953).

70 U.N. CHARTER art. 2, paras. 3 and 4.

71 *Id.*, art. 51.

72 *Id.*, arts. 39, 42.

73 *Id.*, art. 2, para. 5

74 It has been argued that because certain uses of force are permitted by the Charter; and because the rules of war, at least those of humanitarian intent, are recognized by most jurists and by the Geneva Conventions of 1949 as applicable to all parties in all hostilities, war has not been abolished or outlawed. J. KUNZ, THE CHANGING LAW OF NATIONS, p. 855 ff. (1968). These arguments, however, refer to war in the material sense, not to war in the legal sense, the essence of which is the *legal equality* of the belligerents, a distinction recognized expressly by the Supreme Court of the United States (*The Three Friends*, 166 U.S. 1, 57 (1896) and implicitly by the avoidance of the use of the term "war" in the U.N. Charter. It has also been argued that because force has several times been used on a large

44

scale in violation of Charter obligations and Charter sanctions have not been effectively applied; and because the "principle of effectivity" *(fait accompli, ex Factis jus oritur)* must be accepted in the primitive state of international law, the anti-force and collective security provisions of the Charter have become obsolete, and invalid, or at least suspended. (Kunz, *id.* 23, 266, 292, 376 ff., 646 ff., 652, 846 ff., 876, 879). This argument is doubtful in view of the refusal of most states to acquiesce in this interpretation, and, on the contrary, to support the continued effort of the United Nations to realize its principles. In any case the argument applies only to war in the material sense, not to war in the legal sense, the outlawry of which is indicated by the absense declarations of war or recognitions of neutrality, except for states like Switzerland and Austria, with a recognized status of permanent neutrality, in hostilities since World War II. Political Neutralism in the Cold War has not implied legal neutrality in case of aggression. (CHARLES G. FENWICK, INTERNATIONAL LAW, 649, 720 ff. (4th ed. 1965), WILLIAM L. TUNG, INTERNATIONAL LAW IN AN ORGANIZING WORLD, p. 423 ff. 462 (1968), WRIGHT, THE ROLE OF INTERNATIONAL LAW IN THE ELIMINATION OF WAR, 27, 44 ff. (1961).

75 George J. Tomeh, Permanent Representative of Syria in the U.N., 33 *LAW AND CONTEMP. PROB.,* 120 ff. (1968).

76 See statements by permanent representatives to the U.N. from Jordan (El-Farra), U.A.R. (Elaraby), and Syria (Tomeh), *id.,* 68 ff., 103 ff., 120 ff.

77 Fenwick, *op. cit.,* p. 923; WILLIAM W. BISHOP, INTERNATIONAL LAW, CASES AND MATERIALS, 202 (1953). Tung, *op. cit.,* 168.

78 *Cf.* note 59 *supra.*

79 Possession of unclaimed territory *(territorium nullius)* may give good title by the principle of discovery and occupation, but a possessory right to claimed territory established by a cease fire line, while protecting against invasion so long as the cease fire agreement remains valid, does not give title and implies, as did the possessory assizes of Henry II, in 12th century England, that a procedure to determine title should be available. See Williams, *Sovereignty, Seisin and the League,* 7 BRIT. YB. INT'L L. 24, 36-39 (1926); Q. WRIGHT, THE ROLE OF INTERNATIONAL LAW IN THE ELIMINATION OF WAR, 13 (1961). The distinction between a cease fire line and an international boundary was explicitly stated in the 1954 agreement between the French Military Command and Ho Chi Minh which established the cease fire line in Vietnam as a "provisional military demarcation line" and not an "international boundary." The continuing validity of this line was doubtful after withdrawal of one party, France, from the responsibilities it had accepted and violation of the agreement by its successor, Diem. Wright, *Legal Aspects of the Vietnam Situation, supra* note 56, at 756-57.

80 See I J. B. MOORE, INTERNATIONAL LAW DIGEST 297 (1906). The *William Spader* claim (United States v. Venezuela, RALSTON'S REPORT 161 (1904) was not allowed, the Commissioner saying that "a right unasserted for over forty-three years can hardly in justice be called a 'claim'" (*id.* at 161-62), and thirty-two years' prescription was held to bar the *Gentini* claim (Italy v. Venezuela, *id.* at 720). Justice Field, in the U.S. Supreme Court, denied a boundary claim of Virginia against Tennessee on the ground that "a boundary line between States . . . which has been run out, located and marked upon the earth, and afterwards recognized and acquiesced in by the parties for a long course of years, is conclusive, even if it be ascertained that it varies somewhat from the courses given in the original grant . . . ." Virginia v. Tennessee, 148 U.S. 503, 522 (1893); quoted portion in W. BISHOP, INTERNATIONAL LAW: CASES AND MATERIALS 363 (2d. 1962).

81 See Wright, *Custom as a Basis of International Law in the Post-War World,* 2 TEXAS INT'L LAW FORUM 147 (1966); 7 INDIAN J. INT'L L. 1 (1967). Some writers have asserted a principle of "effectivity by which a situation even if originally illegal, may be construed as healed" (Kunz, note 74 *supra* at 266). Unless the conditions of prescription or general recognition are complied with,

this seems difficult to distinguish from the obsolete doctrine of "completed conquest." See note 48 *supra*.

[82] See EVERYMAN'S UNITED NATIONS, *supra* note 22 at 75-76.

[83] Resolution of the Institut de Droit International, Salzburg, Sept. 11, 1961, 49 ANNUAIRE DE L'INSTITUT DE DROIT INTERNATIONAL 370 (1961-II). See also Kansas v. Colorado, 206 U.S. 46 (1907); Wyoming v. Colorado, 259 U.S. 419 (1922); New Jersey v. New York, 283 U.S. 336 (1931); I G. HACKWORTH, DIGEST OF INTERNATIONAL LAW 580-96 (1940).

[84] Georg, Tomeh, *Legal Status of Arab Refugees.* 33 LAW AND CONTEMP. PROB., 110 ff. (1968).

[85] Harvard Research in International Law. *Rights and Duties of States in Case of Aggression* (Philip Jessup, Raporteur), 33 A.M. J. INT'L. (Suppl., 1939) 847; Geneva Conventions, 1949, arts. 2, 3, 75 U.N. Treaty Series, 31, 135, 287.

[86] Note 22 *supra*.

[87] Abba Eban. note 67 *supra*.

[88] Statement by Lawrence Michelmore, Commissioner General for United Nations Relief and Works Administration (UNRWA) in General Assembly, Dec. 1967. GAOR 22 session. sup. no. 13, reported 32 INT. ORG. (Spring 1968) 591 ff., (Summer 1968) 723.

[89] Q. WRIGHT, MANDATES UNDER THE LEAGUE OF NATIONS 327, 462, 468, 528 (1930); Re *Ezra Goralshvih* (Palestine Supreme Court, 1925), unreported, but summarized by the writer in Wright, *Some Recent Cases on the Status of Mandated Territories,* 20 AM. J. INT'L L. 768, 771 (1926).

[90] Protests have been made in the past against gross inhumanities which "shock the conscience of mankind" as did the Leopoldian persecutions in the Congo, and Russian and Hitlerian persecution of Jews even when the injured individuals were subjects of the persecuting state and within its territory. The Nuremberg trials prosecuted individuals for "crimes against humanity," though only when the crimes were in pursuance of illegal war or in violation of the law of war. See Wright, *The Law of the Nuremberg Trial, supra* note 62; E. STOWELL, INTERVENTION IN INTERNATIONAL LAW 51-277 (1922).

[91] "The Universal Declaration of Human Rights," approved by the General Assembly on December 10, 1948 (G. A. Res. 217, 3 U.N. GAOR, pt. 1, Resolution 71, U.N. Doc. A/810 (1948), provides in article 13: "1. Everyone has the right to freedom of movement and residence within the borders of each State. 2. Everyone has the right to leave any country, including his own, and to return to his country." "The International Covenant on Civil and Political Rights," approved by the General Assembly on Dec. 16, 1966 (G. A. Res. 2200, 21 U.N. GAOR, Supp. 16, at 49, U.N. Doc. A/6316 (1966), provides in article 12 (p. 54): "1. Everyone lawfully within the territory of a State shall, within that territory, have the right to liberty of movement and freedom to choose his residence. 2. Everyone shall be free to leave any country, including his own. 3. The above-mentioned rights shall not be subject to any restrictions except those which are provided by law, are necessary to protect national security, public order *(ordre public),* public health or morals, or the rights and freedoms of others, and are consistent with the other rights recognized in the present Covenant. 4. No one shall be arbitrarily deprived of the right to enter his own country."

[92] The German Federal Republic paid reparations to Israel after the Second World War for the destruction and exile of Jews during the Hitler period, some of whom had fled to Palestine. In an interview in March 1968, Nasser said he considered the refugees the most serious Middle Eastern problem. Attwood, *supra* note 31, at 61, 64.

[93] 79 BRIT. & FOR STATE PAPERS 18 (1887-88); 3 AM. J. INT'L L. 123 (Supp. 1909).

[94] U.N. CHARTER, art. 51

95 S.C. Res. 95 (1951); Wright, *Interventions, 1956, supra* note 24 at 261-72.

96 S.C. Res. 118 (1956).

97 36 DEP'T STATE BULL. 387, 390 (1957). Secretary of State Dulles declared in an *aide memoire* to the Israeli Ambassador on February 11, 1957 that "(T)he United States believe that the Gulf comprehends international waters and that no nation has the right to prevent free and innocent passage in the Gulf and through the Straits giving access thereto . . . .
"In the absence of some overriding decision to the contrary, as by the International Court of Justice, the United States, on behalf of vessels of United States registry, is prepared to exercise the right of free and innocent passage and to join with others to secure general recognition of this right." *Id.* at 393.

98 11 U.N. GAOR 1275-76 (1957). See also the position enunciated by Secretary of State Dulles in the General Assembly (U.N. GAOR, 1st Emer. Spec. Sess. 10-12 (1946) introducing the resolution adopted as G.A. Res. 997, *id.* Supp. 1, at 2, U.N. Doc. A/3354 (1956). It called for a cease fire and "urged that upon the cease fire being effective, steps be taken to reopen the Suez Canal and restore secure freedom of navigation." Egypt accepted it "on the condition, of course, that it could not implement the resolution in case attacking armies continued their aggression." *Id.*, Annexes, Agenda Item no. 5, at 3, U.N. Doc. A/3266 (1956). The resolution was adopted against the opposition of Australia, France, Israel, New Zealand, and Great Britain, with abstentions by Belgium, Canada, Laos, Netherlands, Portugal, and South Africa. U.N. GAOR, 1st Emer. Spec. Sess. 34-35 (1956).

99 12 U.N. SCOR, Supp. April-June 1957, at 8, 9, 11, U.N. Doc. S/3818 (1957); (1956-1957) I.C.J.Y.B. 212.

100 Supporters of the Egyptian position emphasize the basic sovereignty of Egypt over the Canal implying an inherent right to defend it in contrast to the merely conventional right of the free passage given by the Convention of 1888. Enjoyment of this right, they insist, is dependent on observance of the obligations of the Convention, especially that of respect for the neutrality of the Canal. Israel, not a party to the Convention, could be a third party beneficiary, only if it accepted these obligations, which, they say, Israel has not done, but on the contrary has attacked Egypt in the Canal area. Consequently, they say, Egypt is entitled to take defense measures. Majid Khadduri, *Closing of the Suez Canal to Israeli Shipping*, 33 LAW AND CONTEMP. PROB., 147 ff. (1968). This argument raises the issue of who was the aggresor in the hostilities of 1949, 1956 and 1967? See section M *infra*.

101 This purpose was indicated in a letter of January 31, 1968 from the Israeli Government to the Secretary-General reiterating its previous refusal to allow the UAR to survey the Canal north of the ships stranded there, and justifying the use of force on the previous day on grounds referred to in the ensuing principle text. U.N. Doc. S/7930/Add. 63, Jan. 31, 1968, at 14-17.

102 N.Y. Times, Jan. 31, 1968, at 1, col. 5.

103 Letter of Jan. 31, 1968, *supra* note 101.

104 Khadduri, note 100 *supra*.

105 Corfu Channel Case, (1949) I.C.J. 4, 28-30. Convention on the Territorial Sea, art. 16(4), (1958) 15 U.S.T. 1606, T.I.A.S. No. 5639; 52 AM. J. INT'L L. 834 (1958).

106 See notes 97 and 98, *supra,* and accompanying text.

107 See Report of the Secretary-General on the withdrawal of the United Nations Emergency Force, U.N. Doc. A/6730/Add. 3, June 26, 1967; 4 U.N. MONTHLY CHRON. No. 7, at 135 (1967).

108 Memorandum cited note 107 *supra,* at paras. 23 and 50.

109 *Id.*, paras. 21, 87-93.

110 Such a power of the Security Council may be inferred in respect to both

47

investigating commissions and peace-keeping forces from articles 25, 29, 34, 40, 104, and 105 of the Charter. 2 REPERTORY OF PRACTICE OF UNITED NATIONS ORGANS art. 29, paras. 17-28; art. 34, paras. 2-14 (1955). See also Q. WRIGHT, INTERNATIONAL LAW AND THE UNITED NATIONS 122 (1960); COMMISSION TO STUDY THE ORGANIZATION OF PEACE, U. N. GUARDS 9 (Spec. Report 1948); CHARTER REVIEW CONFERENCE 32 (9th Report 1948); STRENGTHENING THE UNITED NATIONS 36-38 (10th Report 1957); ORGANIZING PEACE IN THE NUCLEAR AGE 42 (11th Report 1959); NEW DIMENSIONS OF THE UNITED NATIONS 27-28 (17th Report 1966).

111 Wright, *Legal Aspects of the Congo Situation,* 4 INT'L STUDIES: JOURNAL OF THE INDIAN SCHOOL OF INTERNATIONAL STUDIES I, 16-22 (1962).

112 I REPERTORY OF PRACTICE OF UNITED NATIONS ORGANS art. 22, paras. 52, 104-107 (1955); Comm. to Study the Org. of Peace, STRENGTHENING THE UNITED NATIONS, *supra* note 110 at 5, 36, 79.

113 Advisory Opinion on Certain Expenses of the United Nations (Article 17, para. 2, of the Charter), (1962) I.C.J. 151.

114 Yashpal Tandon, UNEF, *The Secretary-General and International Diplomacy in the Third Arab-Israeli War,* 32 INT. ORG. 529 ff. (1968).

115 Wright, *The Stimson Note of January 7, 1932,* 26 AM. J. INT'L L. 342 (1932); LEGAL PROBLEMS IN THE FAR EASTERN CONFLICT 153-56 (1941); *Recognition, Intervention and Ideologies, supra* note 48 at 97.

116 G.A. Res. 997, *supra* note 98.

117 See, *e.g.,* U.N. Doc. S/PV. 1358 (1967).

118 U.N. CHARTER art. 40.

119 *Id.,* arts. 33, 36, 37, 11(2), 14.

120 *Id.,* art. 96.

121 *Id.,* art. 36.

122 *Id.,* art. 94.

123 Withdrawal was demanded in cease fire resolutions pertaining to Kashmir (S.C. Res. 47 (1948), S.C. Res. 209 (1965); Korea (S.C. Res. 82 (1950); and Suez (G. A. Res. 997, *supra* note 82). Withdrawal was not demanded in the case of the Dominican Republic in 1965, nor that of Palestine in 1948, although in the latter situation, S.C. Res. 56 of August 19, 1948 declared that "No party is entitled to gain military or political advantage through violation of the truce."

124 *E.g.,* U.N. Doc. S/PV. 1351, at 21-27, June 8, 1967.

125 Such refusal or violation was considered in League of Nations practice to be the best test of aggression and was incorporated in "The General Convention to Improve the Means of Preventing War," opened for signature on September 26, 1931. 12 LEAGUE OF NATIONS OFF. J., Spec. Supp. 92, at 24 (1931). See also Wright, *The Concept of Aggression in International Law,* 29 AM. J. INT'L L. 373, 382 (1935); *The Prevention of Aggression,* 50 *id.* 514, 530 (1956); A STUDY OF WAR, *supra* note 68. Article 40 of the U.N. Charter contemplates this test. See WRIGHT, THE ROLE OF INTERNATIONAL LAW IN THE ELIMINATION OF WAR, *supra* note 69, at 62.

126 Wright, *The Concept of Aggression in International Law, supra* note 125, at 394.

127 Israel Information Service, N.Y. Bulletin, Feb. 5, 1968. See Notes 97 *supra* and 129 *infra.*

128 See note 125 *supra* and accompanying text.

129 In announcing the withdrawal of Israeli forces from the Aqaba area on March 1, 1957, that country's Foreign Minister said in the General Assembly: "Interference, by armed force, with ships of Israel flag exercising free and innocent

passage in the Gulf of Aqaba and through the Straits of Tiran, will be regarded by Israel as an attack entitling it to exercise its inherent right of self-defence under Article 51 of the United Nations Charter and to take all such measures as are necessary to ensure the free and innocent passage of its ships in the Gulf and in the Straits." II U.N. GAOR 1276 (1957). To similar effect see U.N. Doc. A/PV. 1536, June 19, 1967, at 42-46. An official Egyptian report, published on February 19, 1968, stated that President Nasser warned his close advisers in May 1967 that blockade of the Gulf of Aqaba meant certain war with Israel. N. Y. Times, March 3, 1968, at 12, col. 1.

130 U.N. Doc. S/PV. 1347, June 5, 1967, at 17-21.

131 See remarks of Premier Eshkol quoted in N.Y. Times, July 8, 1967, at 4, col. 4. Israel apologized for its attack on the U.S. intelligence ship *Liberty* on the high seas on June 8, 1967, saying it thought it was an Egyptian ship. N. Y. Times, June 10, 1967, at 14, col. 6. Since the prolonged inspection of the ship by Israeli aircraft and its clear markings make this explanation improbable, it has been suggested that Israel hoped to destroy evidence acquired by the ship of Israel's priority in armed attack on Egypt. LIFE, June 23, 1967, at 29.

132 Statements of the U.A.R. Delegation in the Security Council on May 29 and June 4, 1967, U.N. Docs. S/PV. 1343, at 21-47; S/PV. 1347, at 22-30.

Not only priority in initiating hostilities, but also aggressive intentions and superiority of preparation for attack were considered evidence of the aggressor by the Rumboldt Committee which investigated the Greco-Bulgarian incident of 1925 (see note 133 *infra); by the Lytton Commission which investigated the Manchurian incident of 1931; and by the Nuremberg Tribunal. See Wright, *The Concept of Agression in International Law, supra* note 125 at 380, 386, 388; INTERNATIONAL LAW AND THE UNITED NATIONS, *supra* note 110 at 89. On the Lytton Commission's suggestion that weight in determining the aggressor should be attached to the fact that the Japanese were better prepared than the Chinese when hostilities began on the night of September 18-19, 1931, the writer commented in 1935: "Military efficiency may exhibit some correlation with aggressiveness, but it is doubtful whether the correlation is sufficient to justify the conclusion that the more efficient belligerent is invariably to be branded as the aggressor." *The Concept of Aggression in International Law, supra* note 125, at 381.

133 The principle was applied in art. 232 of the Treaty of Versailles which required Germany to make reparation to Belgium for *all* losses it had suffered as a result of the German invasion in view of Germany's explicit obligation to Belgium under the neutralization treaty of 1839, while reparations to other countries were in principle based on their losses resulting from German violations of the law of war. See Wright, *The Outlawry of War,* 19 AM. J. INT'L L. 76, 86 (1925). See also Articles of Interpretation of the Pact of Paris (Kellogg-Briand Pact): "A violating state is liable to pay compensation for all damage caused by a violation of the Pact to any signatory state or to its nationals." INT'L L. ASS'N, REPORT OF THIRTY-EIGHTH CONFERENCE I, 66, 68 (London 1934). Greece, found to be the aggressor in the Greco-Bulgarian incident of 1925, was required to make reparation for Bulgarian losses. See 37th Sess. of the Council, 12th meeting, 7 LEAGUE OF NATIONS OFF. J. 172 (1925). See also Wright, *The Outlawry of War and the Law of War, supra* note 69.

134 See *Letter,* March 19, 1968 from Mahomed El Kony, Permanent Representative to the U.N. for the U.A.R. (Egypt) to Secretary-General U Thant, quoting statement of Mahmoud Riad, U.A.R. Minister of Foreign Affairs, March 13, 1968 (S/8479, A/7074) and Annual Report of Secretary-General U Thant, 1968 (A/7201, Add. 1, par. 50).

135 Note 67 *supra.*

136 This doctrine, by declaring that "The United States is prepared to use armed force to assist any such (Middle Eastern) nation or group of such nations

49

requesting assistance against armed aggression from any country controlled by international communism" (71 Stat. 5) (1957), convinced the Arab countries, which had just experienced aggression, not from International Communism but from Israel, Great Britain, and France, that the United States had changed its policy which had opposed the latter aggressions. Only Lebanon, under a western-oriented government, among the Arab states accepted the Eisenhower doctrine, and that government was changed by revolution in 1958 partly because of this position conflicting with the Arab policy of "neutralism." See Wright, *United States Intervention in the Lebanon, supra* note 56 at 124. For further discussion of the Eisenhower Doctrine, see 5 M. WHITEMAN, DIGEST OF INTERNATIONAL LAW 1137-56 (1965).

[137] See text accompanying note 26 *supra*. President Eisenhower wrote in his memoirs that the Aswan loan was withdrawn because the Soviet offer was "blackmail" and that arms were refused to Israel to balance those sent to Egypt by the Soviet Union for the same reason. DWIGHT D. EISENHOWER, THE WHITE HOUSE YEARS: WAGING PEACE 1956-1961, at 25, 31 (1965). See also ANTHONY EDEN, FULL CIRCLE 470 (1960).

[138] They professed their solidarity with Israel during the six-day war and appeared to support retention of the occupied areas by Israel, but complained of discrimination in Israel's immigration and welfare policies. See *ISRAEL'S ORIENTAL PROBLEM,* a monthly bulletin distributed by the Council of the Sephardi Community, vol. 3, no. 1, at 4-5 (1967).

[139] *Id.*

[140] *Id.* at 7-8.

[141] *Cf.* notes 15, 17, 59, 60 and accompanying text, *supra.*

PART TWO

*THE FORUM PROCEEDINGS*

# The Forum: A Summary of the Proceedings*

*Professor Fisher*

Professor FISHER'S topic was the implementation of United Nations Resolutions on the Middle East. His major premise was that there has been "too much debate about substantive law and not enough about procedure" in consideration of the Middle East dispute.

While we are likely to think of adjudication when thinking of legal procedures, "the thought of turning the Arab-Israeli conflict over to the International Court of Justice would . . . make even the firmest believer in world peace through law quail."

The process the United Nations is now pursuing in the Middle East is one of negotiation rather than adjudication. This negotiating approach seeks a comprehensive political settlement; it looks toward one "great document" that will deal with all the questions in the Middle East. Several elements of this approach stand out. First, the role of the United Nations is seen as that of a mediator. "The Secretary General's representative, Mr. Jarring, is a 'live post office'." Second, "all the issues are to be dealt with at one time." Third, the parties are expected to maximize their demands so as to give them more room for negotiation. "They are to hold all their cards in their hand." Fourth, each side expects the other to make a major concession first.

In Professor FISHER'S view, this approach holds little hope for success. Both sides currently justify their conduct not in terms of its being a constructive step toward the future but rather in terms of some conduct by the other side in the past. Since there has been "unprincipled conduct" by both sides in the past, little progress can be made by looking backward.

---

* Prepared by Peter M. Mortimer.

The task for a third party institution like the United Nations is "not just to find a result which is acceptable to the parties; it is to effect what they are willing to accept—to exert influence upon them."

"Israel and the Arab states today see the situaion as one single major confrontation. Similarly, the United States and the Soviet Union saw each other during the height of the Cold War as in an all out confrontation.

"Domestically we had the same kind of confrontation between leaders of capital and labor who referred to the "Class War." Today we have those who see all social and domestic questions in terms of a single racial conflict, a confrontation between black and white.

"Now, in the domestic scene we have learned that the wise objective is not to win the Class War or even to negotiate a settlement in the confrontation between the races. It is to break up the conflict into pieces and deal with the pieces.

"Legal techniques and legal experience are crucial in restructuring the perception of a conflict. By having different people and different procedures for dealing with different questions the so-called Class War in this country disappeared over time. It was replaced with a lot of other problems, with different questions.

"Big conflicts are broken up into somewhat more manageable ones. In the relations between the Soviet Union and the United States we are trying to break our way out of the Cold War by dealing with separate problems on the merits.

"The difference between a cold war and a period of peace is not the difference between hate and love. It is whether we see every issue as part of a total confrontation or whether we deal with separate questions on their individual merits. When we can separate the civil aviation agreement with the Soviet Union from the Berlin question, we have reduced the risk of war and we are beginning on our way."

The role, then, of the United Nations, Professor FISHER contended, "is not that of a mediator but more like a chancellor in equity who decides what ought to happen next."

Viewed in this way, the Middle East "problem" should be broken up, with different questions treated separately. Some separable questions are Suez, the Syrian-Israeli border, the status of and access to Jerusalem and the holy places, diplomatic recognition and relations, withdrawal from the Sinai and demilitarization of that border, repatriation, compensation and resettlement of refugees, the Straits of Tiran, and the Jordanian-Israeli boundary.

Applying this approach to the Security Council resolution of November 1967, Professor FISHER suggested that different committees and individuals be assigned to each of the separable questions, with instructions to proceed separately but concurrently. He said that "over time as different working committees or officials were working on different problems, the practical aspect of these problems—where the boundary is, how you demilitarize the Syrian Heights—these begin to loom as more important than ideological confrontation."

"Process is important. Due process is a concept far more fundamental than the interpretation of the Fifth and Fourteenth Amendments to the U.S. Constitution.

"Arab and Jew alike seek justice. The history of law suggests, at least to me, that the justice they seek is more likely to be found by breaking up the present conflict into pieces and dealing with those pieces on their respective merits than in any other way."

### Ambassador Lorch

Ambassador LORCH began by explaining that he was not a lawyer, but rather "a soldier by force of circumstance" and a diplomat "by habit." From this perspective, he commented that "we are still far away from a concept of international relations controlled or governed by the rule of law." "I am afraid," he said, "that the United Nations is not the Supreme Court of this world." "The United Nations, and this is not said in criticism but it is said in a rather sad realization, does not have the impartiality or the objectivity of a court of law."

Further, he noted that "at the moment of our direct peril the United Nations failed to preserve peace and stability in the Middle East." "At a time when the United Nations Emergency Force was most needed, it vanished from the arena." Therefore, he contended, "it would behoove the United Nations to exercise a certain amount of humility and not to pretend to have powers which ultimately it does not have."

Ambassador LORCH then turned to what he called the "political realities" of the Middle East. It is these realities, he contended, that "have determined the shape and the outcome of this crisis." He noted that crises have been a part of history in the Middle East. That area has often been the focal point for the great powers of the times, such as Syria, Babylon, Egypt, Greece, Rome, the Byzantines, the Turks, the Omans, the British, the French, and, today, the Soviet Union and the United States.

Russia's interest in the Middle East, he agreed, was not so much ideological but geographical and political. An example of this, he said, was Mr. Gromyko's statement in the United Nations "that since the Soviet Union is close to the Middle East and by the same token the United States is very far removed from the Middle East, whatever happens in the Mediterranean and Middle East is of direct concern to the Soviet Union and of only indirect concern or no concern to the United States."

The Soviet Union, Ambassador LORCH said, "supported Israel in 1948 not because of the love of Israel but because Israel at that time was engaged in a struggle with the British colonial power which was the major exponent of western interests in the Middle East at that time and later on was engaged in a struggle with Arab countries whose regimes were supported, armed, controlled and led to various degrees by the British." The Soviet Union later abruptly switched its allegiance, he continued, and now supports the Arabs "in order to increase the Soviet presence in the Eastern Mediterranean and then onwards into the Southern Mediterranean."

Ambassador LORCH then discussed the relationship between Soviet presence in the Middle East and the six-day war. "President Nasser said—you don't have to take it from me—President Nasser said that he was prevailed upon to concentrate his forces in the Sinai Peninsula by information received from Soviet sources about a massive concentration of Israeli troops on the Syrian border." Ambassador LORCH said that the Soviet Ambassador had protested this alleged concentration to Mr. Eshkol on the eve of the war, but that the Soviet Ambassador refused Mr. Eshkol's invitation to go to the Syrian border to verify the situation there. He concluded that the Arab-Israeli conflict, in its present dimensions, could not be isolated "from the cold war and the confrontation which does exist between the two super powers" as well as secondary powers that have direct interests in the Middle East.

The Arab countries, he noted, are varied in size, political systems, allegiance, religion, and economic development; they are united only in their hostility to Israel. "That is one of the tragedies of the Middle East and that is why whenever Arabs get together there is a competition of extremism and it is the more extreme who wins." In this way, he contended, public opinion is incited against Israel.

On resolution of the Arab-Israeli conflict Ambassador LORCH said that "the procedure which we envisage and which the United Nations has envisaged in the Security Council Resolution of November 22 is the process of negotiation, agreement, implementation." He stressed the need for Arab willingness "to establish a lasting and permanent peace with Israel." In conclusion, he said, "I am convinced that such a peace will come about. I am convinced moreover that it is in the interest of the Arabs just as much as it is in the interest of Israel and by advocating a permanent and stable peace freely negotiated I am honestly convinced that I am speaking as much as a pro-Arab as a pro-Israeli representative."

*Dr. Dinstein**

Dr. DINSTEIN'S topic was the "Legal Balance of Force and Counter-Force in the Middle East Today." He contended that: "In political terms the problem that is at the root of the interminable tug-of-war in the Middle East is a very simple one: the Arabs wish to put an end to the presence of a Jewish State in the Middle East; Israel, on the other hand, has every intention of enduring. The Arabs, in order to implement their program, use force; Israel, in order to survive, uses counter-force."

The legal problems, however, are more complex. The law of the United Nations Charter forbids the use of force in relations between states except (a) "within the framework of the collective security system established by the United Nations" and (b) "in accordance with Article 51 of the Charter, in self-defense against an armed attack (pending appropriate action by the Security Council)." Since certain phrases used in Article 51, such as "armed attack" and "self-defense," are susceptible of various interpretations, there is controversy over the applicability of that Article to given acts.

"What happens, then, when a State—in violation of its obligations under international law—resorts to the use of force against another? Almost on a daily basis, regular armed units of neighboring Arab countries open fire across the borders of the State of Israel, and bands of marauders attempt to infiltrate through the lines with a view to sowing terror in the country and bringing about its disintegration by way of attrition. It is difficult to deny that these are instances of armed attack against Israel, and the latter is therefore entitled

---

* Since Dr. Dinstein was unable to attend the Forum, this summary is drawn from his paper.

to the use of counter-force by way of self-defense. But what kind of counter-force?"

Dr. DINSTEIN distinguished four types of legitimate uses of counter-force by way of self-defense that may fall within the ambit of Article 51: (1) "Reaction"; (2) Reprisal; (3) "Execution"; and (4) War. For purposes of discussion he put the case of an Israeli patrol moving along the border within its territory and being subjected to intense fire from the other side, with resulting casualties. "The following categories of counter-force in self-defense would then be permissible (until the Security Council has taken the necessary measures to restore the peace)."

"1.   The first category is rather elusive in term since very few lawyers—as distinct from soldiers—take special note of it. For lack of a better name, permit me to call it *Reaction*. That is to say, countering force with force on the spot and on the spur of the moment. In our example, fire would be returned by the patrol, and possibly by immediately support-ing units in that section of the line. The significant charac-teristic of "reaction" is that the exchange of fire closes the incident and does not involve other units at other times.

"2.   *Reprisal*.   That is to say, using force in retaliation for a previous attack by another State. Reprisal is to be dis-tinguished from mere 'reaction' in that an altogether differ-ent incident develops, either with a different unit or at a different time or both. In our example, say that fire would be opened on another day on an enemy patrol, or that a mili-tary base from which the assailants came would be struck. Reprisal, nevertheless, is still a limited response in its scope. inasmuch as it does not entail the use of force *à l'outrance*, and (as laid down by the 1928 Arbitral Award in the *Naulilaa Case*) it has to be proportional to the initial, illegal, use of force by the other side.

"3.   The third category, again, is not always recognized as a mode of counter-action that is independent from others. Occasionally it is called 'necessity,' but I would rather use a

59

different term, namely, *Execution*. That is to say, using force within the territory of another State directed against individuals in retaliation for acts committed by them, on their own responsibility, without the complicity of the Government concerned. 'Execution' is similar to reprisal except that it is not adressed against a Government, and it would usually take place when that Government is unable to control the situation along the border. In our example,, say that the Israeli patrol was attacked not by regular troops of a neighboring Arab country, but rather by a band of marauders unaided by the authorities (obviously, if the bandits are abetted by the authorities, the legal position in terms of governmental responsibility may be equated to the use of regular troops). 'Execution' would take place, for instance, by sending an expeditionary force to annihilate a bandits' camp across the border. The most famous historical precedent for this type of self-defense occurred in 1837, when Canadian troops crossed the American border and destroyed the steamship, *The Caroline,* used by unauthorized individuals to support rebels in Canada.

"4. *War.* That is to say, a full-scale use of counterforce, which is total in character. Unlike reprisal, war does not at all have to be proportional to the original use of force by the enemy. It is of the essence of war that (subject to the rules of conduct in warfare) everything is permitted in it to bring about the overall destruction of the enemy. By way of example, after Pearl Harbor the United States could, and did, seek unconditional surrender of the enemy, and not merely retribution for the blow to its naval power."

Dr. DINSTEIN suggested, however, "on the basis of international theory and practice, that full-scale war in self-defense may be unleashed in response to an isolated instance of use of force only when justified by a reasonable combination of urgency and necessity." Further, "recourse to war in self-defense is a right and not a duty." Even when an attack by one State on another justifies war as a response in self-

60

defense, the attacked State may choose not to exercise its right. The latter may, instead, have recourse to reprisal.

Dr. DINSTEIN concluded his remarks by observing:

"Being subjected incessantly to new armed attacks by neighboring Arab countries, the State of Israel in effect faces almost daily the option whether to respond to force with counter-force, and, if so, whether the response should be of the type of 'Reaction,' 'Reprisal,' 'Execution' or War. If the option since June 1967 has been exercised in such a way that repetition of war has been avoided, this is simply due to what cynics may term 'the triumph of hope over experience.' But in the long run another big war in the Middle East cannot be averted unless an end is put to the small war that goes on all the time. For the human being who gets killed there is no difference whether it happens in real war or in what lawyers may dub a *'status mixtus.'* Peace, as pointed out by Litvinov a generation ago, is indivisible."

### Mr. McCloy

Mr. McCLOY began his discussion by stressing the urgent need to deal "promptly and objectively" with the problems of the Middle East. "I think we have allowed it to drift too long," he said, and asserted that "it is the chief imperative of our statesmanship today to cope with this problem."

Mr. McCLOY noted that while there is a tendency by some "to minimize the significance of this part of the world," the Middle East "probably is at least as great a potential source of trouble, of danger, and combines a greater concentration of strategic factors than most other areas in the world."

He observed that: "It is not only in the national interest but in the interests of our Allies in Western Europe to deal constructively with this problem. Indeed, the peace of the world may well be involved by what transpires in this Middle East area.

"The situation transcends the issues between two individual countries or groups of peoples. Their interests are im-

61

portant but they cannot be treated in isolation and as simply a dispute between the Arabs and the Israeli.

"We must try to achieve as best we can a just solution between the Arabs and the Israeli. Yet there are other influences which are of extreme importance not only to the Arabs and the Israeli but to the rest of the world and because they are of such importance to the rest of the world they impel moderation on the part of the Arabs and the Israeli themselves."

Mr. McCLOY then said that he was "very encouraged about the existence of possible solutions" as a result of his trip to the Middle East in the spring of 1968, during which he met with President Nasser, King Hussein and King Faisal.

Taking issue with Professor Fisher as to the desirability of fragmenting the Middle East problem, Mr. McCLOY said that "there are certain fundamentals and there is a certain grouping of problems which I believe point to the possibility and the wisdom of dealing with the complex of problems as a whole." He went on to state that the November, 1967 Security Council Resolution contains important and fundamental principles which can lead to a peaceful settlement. Certain steps might be taken which could be supported by both sides, such as the demilitarization of the Sinai and of the Western bank of the Jordan, the opening of the Straits of Tiran, and the renewal of efforts to relieve the condition of the refugees.

As to demilitarization, Mr. McCLOY said there should be "a simultaneous and concurrent implementation of the security measures and the withdrawals." He quoted President Nasser as talking of a "package deal" and agreed that this would be the appropriate procedure. He found that the Arab leaders desired peace and were prepared to end the state of belligerency.

Mr. McCLOY also related Arab attitudes on particular problems, such as the opening of the Suez Canal. "Mr. Nasser indicated to me that one of the things that he feared about opening the Suez Canal was the likelihood of sabotage or the difficulty an Israeli ship with an Israeli flag might encounter going through the canal. The flow of cargoes, including Israeli cargoes through the canal on other ships, was something that he could contemplate immediately if other parts of 'the package' were agreed on."

Finally, Mr. McCLOY emphasized that the Great Powers involved in establishing the State of Israel have a responsibility to bring about a peaceful solution of the Middle East conflict. He said, "it may be that this will require some twisting of arms but some reasonable pressure is not going to break anybody's arm and if it brings about peace, who should complain?"

### Ambassador El-Erian

Ambassador EL-ERIAN'S topic of discussion was "the responsibility of the United Nations vis-a-vis a peaceful settlement of the Palestine question." Noting that the United Nations had been concerned with this question in various ways for many years, he said that the "problem of Palestine" is special. "It does not involve a dispute between two states on a difference of interpretation or application of a treaty or on adjustment of a frontier or on any other problems which could be brought before the United Nations. It relates to basic laws of the Charter and of contemporary international law. It relates to a right of the whole people to self-determination from the basic principle of the Charter. It relates to one of the basic injunctions of the Charter, the provision of the use of force, and it relates to the principal papers of the organization and its primary function, the maintenance of peace and security."

Ambassador EL-ERIAN maintained that the United Nations' responsibility in the Middle East was not an academic question. "It has its bearing on the interpretation and implementation of Resolution 242, which is the basis for a peaceful settlement of the situation which arose out of the armored attack of a member state of the United Nations

63

against three member states, and the illegal occupation of their territory by force."

Contrasting the statement of the foreign ministers of Israel and the United Arab Republic, Ambassador EL-ERIAN found a basic difference of interpretation: "One side considers the resolution as a framework for direct negotiations and the other side considers that the resolution provides for an integrated, overall settlement through the United Nations, under the supervision of the United Nations and with the guarantee of the United Nations."

Before further considering the United Nations' role in implementing Security Council Resolution 242, Ambassador EL-ERIAN discussed "constitutional" and "organizational" aspects of the United Nations' responsibility in the Middle East.

With respect to constitutional aspects, he cited Article 22 of the Covenant of the League of Nations and Article 80 of the Charter and argued that "the legal action that was open to the General Assembly in 1947 was either to place the mandate of Palestine under trusteeship or to declare its independence." The General Assembly, however, he said recommended partition of Palestine without enlisting the exercise of a right of self-determination, the feeling of the expressed will of the overwhelming majority of the people of Palestine." He also mentioned as a basic constitutional instrument General Assembly Resolution 194 of December 11, 1948, which recognized certain rights of Arab refugees.

With respect to organizational aspect, Ambassador EL-ERIAN mentioned the Conciliation Commission and the Truce Supervision Commission.

Turning finally to the Security Council Resolution 242, Ambassador EL-ERIAN argued that it could not be seen as merely establishing a framework for direct negotiation between the parties. The implementation of the resolution, he said, should be through the United Nations. "This is not a dispute between two states. This is a situation, a breach of

64

the peace and a threat to the peace, and the United Nations must discharge its responsibility and must finalize the peaceful settlement of this dispute. The United Nations has a challenge to meet. It has a responsibility to discharge and it has a promise to fulfill. It can turn what has been a measure of disappointment into a solid achievement and it can pave the road to a real, genuine, just and lasting peace in the area, which the area needs badly, so that we may proceed with the problems of economic development and social progress."

Ambassador EL-ERIAN observed: "The United Nations passes through a crisis. There is a feeling that it is not an effective instrument for the maintenance of international peace and security. The Middle East problem presents the United Nations with an opportunity to settle this problem and to supervise its implementation and to guarantee it."

In conclusion, he said "It is, therefore, the earnest hope of all people who long for a rule of law among the nations, and for the respect of the basic principles of the Charter, that the United Nations meet that challenge in the Middle East and discharge its responsibility and fulfill the promise."

## Ambassador El-Farra

Ambassador EL-FARRA spoke on "two aspects of the Middle East crisis": "the legality of the Israeli military occupation of Arab territories" and "Israeli measures of repression and the people's resistance."

As to the first aspect, Ambassador EL-FARRA concluded, "it is axiomatic that by an illegal act, no legal result can be produced, no right acquired. There can be no fruits for aggression." In support of this principle he cited General Assembly Resolutions 997 (ES-I), 999 (ES-I), and 1002 (ES-I); a statement by Henry Cabot Lodge before the General Assembly on March 1, 1957; the "Stimson Doctrine" of 1932; the Buenos Aires Declaration of 1936; the Lima Declaration of 1938; and Article 17 of the Charter of the Organization of American States.

Ambassador EL-FARRA then considered the meaning and scope of Security Council Resolution 242 of November 22, 1967. Noting the point made by Professor Wright that the November resolution called for withdrawal of Israeli forces from territories occupied in the recent conflict "without specifying whether this meant all such territory as demanded by the Arabs," Ambassador EL-FARRA contended that the meaning of the resolution is clear:

"Withdrawal covers every single inch of territory occupied by force, otherwise a basic principle of international law, embodied in the preamble of the resolution, emphasizing the inadmissibility of acquisition of territory by war, would be grossly violated.

"Violation of this basic principle, I submit, was never the intention of the Security Council. Any other interpretation would amount to justifying acquisition by force and we know that military supremacy cannot create new rights where none existed previously."

Ambassador EL-FARRA then stated that although "the Israelis have claimed that Jerusalem was excluded" from the November resolution, "this contention was rejected by the Security Council in its resolution on the question of Jerusalem" (S.C. Res. 252). He noted that this resolution "again incorporated the principle that there can be no acquisition of territory by military conquest and 'urgently called upon Israel to rescind all such measures already taken and to desist forthwith from taking any further action which tends to change the status of Jerusalem'."

"If we assumed, for the sake of argument, that the November resolution is vague regarding any part of the occupied territory, I submit that the Jerusalem resolution clarifies that vagueness."

As to the second aspect of the Middle East conflict chosen by Ambassador EL-FARRA for discussion—"Israeli measures of repression and the people's resistance"—he contended: "the Israeli occupation has denied the people all of their

66

basic rights including their right to self-determination and expression. Resistance is the only course open to them to challenge the Israeli aggression."

He stated that "no matter what view we take of the situation, the following facts stand clear:

"Number 1. That there is an Arab territory occupied by foreign forces.

"Number 2. That there is a decision calling for withdrawal.

"Number 3. That Israel not only refuses to withdraw but has established Jewish settlements on Arab lands within the occupied area; that it resorts to all forms of oppression to perpetuate its illegal occupation.

"Number 4. That, in the United Nations, there are forces that substitute political expediency for the rule of law and, therefore, no effective measures can be taken in accordance with Chapter VII of the Charter to remedy the situation.

"Number 5. That these factors, the occupation, the inaction, the arbitrary measures, the political expendiency, all lead to one conclusion, namely, resistance."

Ambassador EL-FARRA concluded, however, that peace "can be achieved by honouring all past and present United Nations obligations, all resolutions and all instruments signed by the parties." He closed his remarks by disagreeing with Mr. Engel over the question of Arab negotiations with the Israelis. He cited past commitments and promises which the Israelis did not honour, such as the Protocol of Lausanne of 12 May 1949, and concluded that the prospects for peace are there, but Israel is not genuinely interested in peace and has rather chosen territorial expansion.

## Mr. Engel

Mr. ENGEL noted that while the Hammarskjöld forums are described as a series of case studies on the role of law in the settlement of international disputes, he felt that law had "played very little, if any, role in the Middle East." In his opinion, the law applicable to the Middle East is contained in two basic documents: the United Nations Charter and the Partition Resolution of November, 1947. As to the Partition Resolution he asserted that "the Israelis were keenly disappointed in several aspects of the plan but, for the sake of peace, they accepted the Resolution and offered to live in friendship and brotherhood with the Arab States."

"The Arabs ignored this offer. In defiance of the Partition Resolution and in violation of the provisions of the U.N. Charter, they attacked, for the declared purpose of driving Israel into the sea."

Mr. ENGEL then outlined the current Israeli position as stated by Mr. Eban. This position is based on two central issues: "the establishment of a permanent peace" and "an agreement on the delineation of secure and recognized boundaries." On specific questions, he noted Mr. Eban's proposals for security arrangements to prevent recurrence of hostilities, for the establishment of open frontiers and freedom of navigation in area waterways, for a conference to attempt to solve the refugee problem on the basis of a "five-year plan," for a solution to control of Jerusalem holy places, and for regional cooperation on common problems in the Middle East. Finally, he noted that Israel has cooperated with Ambassador Jarring and no longer insists on direct negotiation.

Mr. ENGEL then discussed the Arab position.

"The position of the Arabs is that the Security Council Resolution of November, 1967 directs Israel to withdraw from the occupied territories and that there can be no discussion until a withdrawal takes place.

"In insisting on adherence to this one provision the Arabs ignore the fact that it is one of five included in the resolution and the second of these calls for termination of the state of belligerency and acknowledgment of the sovereignty, territorial integrity and political independence of every state in the area and their 'right to live in peace within secure and recognized boundaries free from threats or acts of force'."

He further characterized the Arab position as intransigent and quoted the "formula put forth at the Khartoum summit conference in July 1967: 'No recognition, no negotiations, no peace.'"

Turning to the situation as of June 4, 1967, Mr. ENGEL asserted that Egypt had taken the following steps "for the declared purpose of initiating a war to achieve the destruction of Israel:

"First.   She had brought about the removal of the United Nations Emergency Force, which had maintained peace on that frontier for a decade.

"Second.   She had moved 100,000 troops and 900 tanks through the Sinai Peninsula to the Israeli border.

"Third.   She had transferred part of her air force to advance bases in the Sinai Peninsula, where they were within seven and a half minutes flying time from Tel Aviv.

"Fourth.   She had declared a blockade of the Gulf of Aqaba, which had become one of Israel's lifelines. Not only is such a blockade recognized by international law as an act of war but it was specifically declared to be such by Nasser himself on May 22, 1967."

He contended that other hostile acts were taken by Syria and Jordan.

Mr. ENGEL then discussed the question of "the occupied countries and the treatment of the Arabs by Israel." His essential conclusion was that the Israeli occupation has been "enlightened" and that "there has been a return to normalcy in the occupied areas, which are now under civilian control."

On the question of the Arab refugees, Mr. ENGEL contended that "Israel has made attempts in various directions to help solve this problem, but the Arabs so far have shown themselves unwilling to do their share in this immense task."

Turning to the future, Mr. ENGEL said that Israel cannot concede to Arab demands "without receiving in return at least an acknowledgment of her right to exist in peace and security." He concluded that if this were done, and if the

Arabs would negotiate with Israel, "directly or indirectly," peace could be achieved. He listed the following as benefits that would flow from peace:

"First, secure and recognized boundaries arrived at by negotiations, direct or indirect.

"Second, non-aggression pacts between Israel and each of its Arab neighbors, guaranteed, if desired, by the great powers and by the United Nations.

"Third, an end to the use of force and threats of force by either side.

"Fourth, an end to the tragic loss of life and property which we have seen over the past twenty years.

"Fifth, use of the huge sums now going into armaments to improve the standard of living of the masses on both sides.

"Sixth, collaboration between Israel and its neighbors in a joint campaign to eliminate poverty, ignorance and disease throughout the Middle East."

## Mr. Schwebel*

Mr. SCHWEBEL said that he would speak on five of the thirteen legal problems treated by Professor Wright in the working paper. He explained, "On the questions I shall consider, I believe that Israel has a strong case. But let me say that, of course, I recognize that, in the Palestine problem as a whole, both the law and the equities are mixed. In particular, the profound sense of grievance felt by the Arabs is understandable—and must be understood."

The first question discussed by Mr. SCHWEBEL was the legality of the partition of Palestine. He noted Professor Wright's conclusion that partition was of doubtful legality since the General Assembly's resolution ignored Article 80 of the Charter. He also noted Ambassador El-Farra's and Ambassador El-Erian's view that the partition was clearly illegal

---

* Mr. Schwebel prefaced his remarks by stating that while he is an officer of the American Society of International Law, he does not speak for it.

as a violation of principles of self-determination for the people of Palestine.

Taking issue with Professor Wright's conclusion, Mr. SCHWEBEL contended that Article 80 "is not relevant to what the General Assembly was charged with doing in recommending partition." Article 80 is contained in the International Trusteeship System Chapter of the Charter and provides that: "Except as may be agreed upon in individual trusteeship agreements...nothing in this Chapter shall be so construed in or of itself to alter in any manner the rights whatsoever of any states or any peoples or the terms of existing international instruments to which Members of the United Nations may respectively be parties."

Mr. SCHWEBEL said that "In adopting the partition resolution, the General Assembly did not operate under the trusteeship chapter of the Charter. It acted under Articles 10 and 14, which give it the authority to discuss questions within the scope of the Charter and to recommend measures for the peaceful adjustment of any situation.

"The General Assembly construed nothing in the trusteeship chapter as of itself altering the rights referred to in Article 80. Accordingly, it did not transgress Article 80, which, in any event, is merely a 'saving clause'."

The Assembly's action terminating the mandate, he noted, was taken in response to the United Kingdom's request to "the Assembly to make recommendations under Article 10 of the Charter, concerning the future government of Palestine." He concluded that the request of the United Kingdom was "legally well founded" and cited as authority and precedent the International Court of Justice's Advisory Opinion on the *International Status of South West Africa* ([1950] I.C.J. 141-144), and the United Nations' action with respect to Trieste, the former Italian colonies and New Guinea.

Mr. SCHWEBEL called the argument that the partition plan violated right of self-determination "plausible but defective" because it is based "on the assumption that the principle

71

of self-determination could be applied to Palestine only as an undivided territorial unit." Referring to Elihu Lauterpacht's pamphlet, "Jerusalem and the Holy Place," he argued that self-determination is applicable to sections of a country. To support this point, he mentioned the division of the former mandate of French Togoland into Ghana and Togo and the case of the German Cameroons. He quoted Mr. Lauterpacht's assertion that the partition of Palestine, "far from being a denial of the right of self-determination, was in fact a direct application of the principle. The Jews were not to determine the future of the Arabs, nor were the Arabs to determine the future of the Jews. Each was to determine its own future. This the Jews subsequently did. The Arabs of Palestine did not." The fact that the Arabs did not accept the Assembly's resolution, Mr. SCHWEBEL said, did not invalidate it.

The second question asked by Mr. SCHWEBEL was, "Who was the aggressor in the six-days' war?" The United Arab Republic's closure of the Gulf of Aqaba to Israeli ships, he said, was the first act of force and one commonly regarded as an act of war. Israel was entitled to use force in self-defense. The further question was, whether or not that use of force was proportionate.

Mr. SCHWEBEL noted that "Egyptian provocation" was not confined to the Gulf, large forces had been massed in Gaza and Sinai and the United Nations Emergency Force had been withdrawn on Egyptian demand. Nasser was threatening the use of force.

"In the circumstances, he said, "it may be argued that Israel could not be expected to offer a modest armed challenge in the Gulf of Aqaba knowing that it would likely trigger a major Egyptian first strike from Gaza and Sinai towards Israel's heartland as well as the bombing of Israel's cities." He added that the United Nations, which "has not traditionally manifested tenderness for Israeli retaliatory and pre-emptive measures," did not condemn Israeli actions in connection with the six-days' war. He concluded that "If—

taking all the foregoing considerations into account—Israel was not an aggressor, it would seem to follow that it acted in lawful self-defense."

The third question discussed by Mr. SCHWEBEL was, "Is continued Israeli occupation of Arab territory lawful?" As to the initial occupation, he said that it "appears to be lawful, if it is accepted that it came about as a part of wider, essentially defensive measures." As to the continued occupation, he made three points:

"First, Israel has not purported to acquire territory by war or even defensive action; there is a great difference between temporary occupation and dispositive annexation.

"Second, the Security Council clearly ties withdrawal by Israel to a radical reformation of the belligerent policies which the Arab states have maintained against Israel since its birth.

"Third, the Council's resolution takes care to speak of Israeli withdrawal 'from territories of recent conflict'—not from 'all' territories of recent conflict. It leaves room for border adjustments."

He concluded that: "If the Arab states insist on maintaining that they are in a state of war, they must be prepared to suffer the consequences of the most favorable defensive posture by the state on which they war; when they are prepared to make peace, withdrawal of Israeli forces obviously must be an element of that peace."

The fourth question raised by Mr. Schwebel was, "Are the measures taken by Israel to change the status of the old city of Jerusalem unlawful?" While he noted that the General Assembly twice called such measures unlawful and asked for their rescission, he contended that there was a plausible case to the contrary. That case is based on the proposition that the original Jordanian attack on Jewish inhabitants of Jerusalem during the invasion of Palestine "gave rise to no good title." Since Israeli presence in the new city of Jerusalem was "defensive and not illegitimate," and since the

73

United Nations' efforts to internationalize Jerusalem were gradually abandoned, Israeli forces acting in self-defense during the six-days' war did not enter on to territory as to which Jordan had good title. "As against Jordan, therefore, Israeli title in old Jerusalem is superior. As against the United Nations, the situation is less clear, but it is significant that, in its 1967 resolutions, the General Assembly does not assert Jerusalem is or should be internationalized."

The fifth and final question discussed by Mr. SCHWEBEL was, "is the policy of belligerency of the Arab States lawful?" His short answer, citing Article 2, paragraphs 3 and 4 of the Charter and "accepted United Nations law that the non-recognition by a state of another state which exists *de facto* does not entitle the former to attack or threaten the latter," was "No." "The Arab states understandably resent the creation of Israel. But virtually all the world except the Arab states accepts the fact that Israel is a state and a member of the United Nations, and thereby is entitled to the protection of international law. Until the Arab states equally accept that fact, and apply that law, prospects for peace in the Middle East will remain poor."

## Questions from the Audience

### DECEMBER 4, 1968

Question: I would like to ask Mr. McCloy whether he thinks direct meetings between the Israelis and Arabs are necessary for a package solution.

Mr. McCLOY: I don't think that at the initial stages they are necessary.

You may say that the Arabs are very obdurate about this. Some of them are not.

Again, I can't commit any of the statesmen with whom I talked, but I did get intimations that some were more gunshy of sitting down with the Israelis and working out a plan, but there are ways.

Again, drawing on your legal experience, you can deposit your documents in escrow and they are just as binding, just as legal, awkward perhaps. You don't have the interchange and the face to face confrontation at the beginning of the negotiations, but it is a situation which isn't impossible to work out.

I do think for one reason or another, I must say I don't understand all the reasons in connection with it, but there is a good bit of passion and a good bit of feeling in connection with it all, but I have a feeling that there are techniques that could be worked out through a mediator.

It would be absolutely legal, just as solid a peace settlement as if it were the convention form of around the table signing of one particular document.

Question: Professor Fisher, I think your approach is based upon the assumption that in fact breaking it up into pieces, a legal approach has in fact worked and I think many serious people would doubt whether in fact the legal approach has worked in this country on the racial question and whether in fact it would work in the Middle East.

Mr. FISHER: There are two objectives at any one time, one is victory and one is peace. If a particular party has a strong social view as to what he wants the result to be, and he wants it in a hurry, he may have to use force. He will then have fighting and perhaps victory, but no peace.

We have a situation where we have plenty of conflict and not enough settlement. I think that settlement piece by piece is far superior to a race riot.

I think it is intriguing we have had non-compliance on the school case without out-and-out civil war.

I would like to indicate I don't think Mr. McCloy and I are in much disagreement about a "package deal". I take it to be the resolution of the Security Council that all states shall be secure and accepted, that there shall be no keeping of territories obtained by force, that there should be withdrawal from the territories back to the 1967 lines and so forth.

We have one resolution which has everything on it now, one set of principles. I think that is the package we can't break up.

I think we can go from that right on to developing some documents that deal with parts of the problem. Mr. McCloy has already broken off six pieces, the Syrian heights, and the refugees and other problems. And I would not say we must deal with these one at a time except they don't all have to be on the same piece of paper at the same time.

Question: The question is directed to Ambassador Lorch. Prior to the June war it was expected that the United States government would take more decisive action to avert the possibility of war and the then administration did almost nothing.

Can you tell us what the present position of the Israeli government would be towards the President-elect regarding the future problem and future conflict arising in the same way?

AMBASSADOR LORCH: Were you speaking about the Israeli administration or the American administration?

Question: The Israeli administration anticipated some direct action would be taken by the American government. Then there was a statement through the State Department that the U. S. was neutral in thought, act and deed and eventually nothing did happen on the part of the administration.

Now as Ambassador McCloy has mentioned, there is presently a mission that has gone to the Middle East.

My question to you is, does the Israeli government have any position towards the new American government regarding a future conflict?

AMBASSADOR LORCH: The question is what is it that Israel would like, is that right, the future American administration to do about the Middle East?

I don't want to go into the details of the Israel and American relations but I will say this, that we should hope that any future American administration would continue along the broad lines of the policy of the present government which has been expressed in the five points of President Johnson on June 19, 1967.

I think they have been recapitaluted to a very large extent by Mr. McCloy here tonight, and that is that the search for a permanent peace in the Middle East must continue.

Now, there have been differences of opinion. There always are differences of opinion between friendly governments and where one is not in the position to dictate to the other. That is part of the process but they have always differed on details and not on the essentials.

Let me make it quite clear. We have never asked for American boys to fight in the Middle East and I hope and pray to God that we never shall.

What we have asked the American government to do is to provide Israel with or to enable Israel to buy those arms which it requires in order to offset the tremendous influx of armaments from the Soviet Union into the Arab countries.

I say tremendous because today the Egyptian air force is way above and beyond what it used to be before June, 1967.

The Soviet Union sent arms gratis to them.

We asked for the opportunity to buy arms from the United States. We do hope that such opportunities will be open and we are quite confident that that is possibly the only way, simply a major route to avoiding a situation in which the United States will be called upon to take a direct role in Middle Eastern war.

Moreover we are convinced that a weak Israel would be an invitation to war. The Arabs would not have done what they did in June 1967 unless they believed that they were ready for an all out war.

Thank God they were mistaken but that was their belief and that belief has been expressed very openly by President Nasser in May, 1967.

If I may be permitted one remark about what my predecessor here said. To us direct negotiations are the acid test of the willingness to recognize Israel and that is why we have been rather obstinate about direct negotiations although we have agreed to discuss certain matters of substance indirectly and we are doing that.

Unfortunately we have quite often over the last twenty years had occasion to confirm Mr. McCloy and others, telling us what the Arabs think but we have failed to hear any Arab say openly, all right we are willing to stop this nonsense and recognize you; whether we like it or not Israel is here and Israel is here to stay.

They always have a way of saying something privately to certain visitors, particularly to those from the United States, and saying something else publicly to their own people but ultimately any agreement which is not supported by public opinion in the Arab countries will not stand. Therefore we consider it important for Arab leaders to have to say to their people, we are sorry, we have to change that position, and not to say publicly to their own people, no peace, no recognition, no negotiation and then say what Mr. McCloy has told us and I am quite convinced that very faithfully this is the situation we have had so long and it is the route of disaster.

Here one has to be rather obstinate. The Arab leaders are the only ones who can tell their own people that Israel is there to stay whether they like it or not.—We don't say that there must be public diplomacy but there must be public acceptance of any agreement which ultimately can be reached.

Now, there are certain differences but I am honestly convinced that the basic aims of American diplomacy and Israeli diplomacy in the Middle East are the same and will continue to be the same in the future.

## December 5, 1968

CYRUS ABBIE: This is addressed to Professor Schwebel.

Professor Schwebel, what happens to the doctrine of proportionality if you consider not only the initial attack versus the response, but you also start to consider the state of armaments of the country that is doing the initial attacking? Isn't is likely that in almost any international violation you are going to have a country arming itself as strongly as possible against a country and moving its forces through that state in expectation of some sort of possible response that might come?

And if you take this into consideration in determining where you are going to allow proportionality, aren't you really going to destroy the doctrine of proportionality and, therefore, have continual escalation between two sides that are face to face with war?

What I have been trying to suggest is, if you take into consideration not only the initial violation in determining how far the second country can go, but the state of armaments of the first country, instead of discouraging greater and greater attacks back and forth between countries you are going to be encouraging such attacks.

Mr. SCHWEBEL: I think the first point is well taken. I would not suggest that proportionality can be determined by the sole criterion of the state of preparedness of the country that first commits a violation as against which the second country reacts.

In the case of the June, 1967 war, there were a multiplicity of factors which I think should be taken into account in assessing whether Israel's reaction was proportionate or not.

As I indicated in my remarks, I think a question can be raised about its proportionality. At the same time, it was not only the fact that Egypt was in complete mobilization on Israel's borders, but that bellicose utterances, to put it mildly, came from the United Arab Republic and other Arab states. There was the Arab refusal to accept information as being accurate emanating from United Nations sources to the effect that there was no Israeli massing on the Syrian frontier; and the refusal of the informants of the Arabs, notably the Russians, to accept the invitation of the Israelis to tour the border to see if their charges were true. And what may be assumed to be the appreciation on the part of the United Arab Republic that Israel could not accept closure of the Straits of Tiran should have been plain before closure was invoked.

Putting all that together, the question of proportionality is not easily resolved. I suggest it is not an open and shut case by any means against Israel.

Mr. LOUIS BIRMAN: My question is addressed to Ambassador El-Erian.

I would like to know whether recognition of Israel as a state with perhaps boundaries coinciding with what they were in 1949 is, in your opinion, compatible with genuine bilateral negotiations directed toward achieving a permanent peace?

AMBASSADOR EL-ERIAN: I think the question should be divided into two parts. The first part can be easily replied to.

We accepted all provisions of the Security Council as an integrated solution or as a package deal. Among these resolutions is acknowledgement of the right of every state to live in peace.

The question of borders is another question. I do not agree with Professor Schwebel that the resolution did not state that it covers all territoies — I do not agree with this.

It must be interpreted, as Ambassador El-Farra has pointed out, in light of the basic principles of non-admissibility of territorial gain through war.

I don't think the security of boundaries means that you annex more boundaries. The security will come when you have a peaceful settlement, when the nature of the relationship between the two sides are changed, but I don't think that expansion and adding will guarantee security.

That is why the expansion should be rejected, because it is against the basic laws of the Charter.

Mr. ROGER FISHER: I would like to make some remarks.

We are talking about the role of lawyers. One role is as advocates. We have heard good advocacy tonight for some past causes never more brilliantly put than Steve Schwebel did on some fine legal points.

Ambassador El-Farra presented a good legal case for the right of resistance.

We have had other arguments as we as lawyers would give them to a court if we were in court.

The point I tried to make last night is that there is another role for lawyers and that is resolving disputes and moving forward. I must say that I was disappointed tonight.

I was particularly disappointed that after Ambassador El-Erian had stated categorically that the UAR had accepted every aspect of the Security Council resolution of last November, and read the points, including the security of boundaries, and access to the waters, Mr. Engel then quoted statements made some years ago when the Arabs were not adopting that position.

It is not surprising that the Arabs feel they don't get a fair hearing if within five minutes after taking a position of full compliance with a mandatory Security Council resolution and referring to the various elements of it that position is ignored and we hear an extreme advocate argue the way you or I might argue a case hoping to compromise somewhere in between. Let me ignore that statement in turn.

Looking forward, I don't think there is so much difference between Mr. McCloy's package deal and what I was talking about with regard to fragmentation. I am talking about a package deal in implementing the Security Council resolution. The decision is outlined there. The essential terms are right there. Demilitarization of some areas, withdrawal, international observation, waterways, refugees and so forth.

The Arabs have criticized Israel for not "accepting" this resolution. Israel doesn't have to accept it. It is a mandatory resolution of the Security Council and it should be implemented whether it is acceptd or not. It is not for Israel to reject. It should be implemented.

Some things will be lumped. Obviously, the relationship

81

between withdrawal and demilitarization of a given area has to be put together. The Sinai demilitarization does not, however, have to be related to the Syrian one, and the water rights of the Jordan River and the settlement of refugees do not have to be tied in with the Gulf of Aqaba.

I think we cannot implement something without getting to work on it. I believe that there are about a half dozen different parts of this resolution which can be pushed ahead simultaneously.

The question is to devise some operative document. What would you draft? What is the next piece of paper that somebody would have to sign in order to get something done? Would it be a "clear the canal" piece of paper to be initialed, or what?

Let us get on with the lawyer-like task of looking ahead. God knows, there are enough problems there. We could argue old issues forever. We should learn that there is little profit in looking at the worst that each adversary has said about the other. There is a good deal to be gained through building on the most promising statements they have made and in a lawyer-like way getting on to the next step, the next operational piece of paper.

Mr. MORRIS PROSKAUER: That was a brilliant statement made by Professor Fisher with regard to what a lawyer can do. It seems to overlook one simple fact.

We lawyers can be effective if there is communication on both sides.

My question to you, sir, since you have raised this issue is, with whom will the Israelis communicate if the Arabs refuse to talk to them?

Mr. FISHER: Mr. Jarring is ready, willing and able to talk substance. For a year the Arabs have suggested that substantive implementation take place. The Secretary General reported to the Security Council this fall that one side was prepared to talk substance and the other side wished first to have the satisfaction that would come from an official hand shaking—a kiss-and-make-up sort of recognition—that would get that point on the table first.

The Arabs have said, "You withdraw first and get that out of the way and then we will come to the other problems."

The Israelis, as I said, are saying, "Let us settle our legitimate status first and then we can get on to the other problems."

There are people to talk to. The United Nations is ready to talk.

Mr. McCloy indicated that the United States government could play a more active role. The Discussions are quite possible if they were not being delayed in part, as I understand the situation, by the desire that the forum for the talks be one which would confer legitimacy and recognition. This is certainly part of the whole package, but it need not be the first item on the agenda.

Mr. ENGEL: I have been allowed exactly one minute. In that one minute I want to say this:

I think I tried, and I hope I did succeed, in making it clear that what I was appealing for was peace and how peace could be achieved. I said that peace could only be achieved if Israel were given recognition; if the formula adopted by the Arab leaders in Khartoum of "no recognition, no negotiations, no peace" was dropped.

I don't see how it can be argued that the Arabs have been willing to negotiate when they constantly have reiterated that proposition. If they are willing to change and begin to negotiate then I think progress can be made toward peace, and I certainly for one would rejoice if that were done.

*SELECTED BIBLIOGRAPHY*

# Selected Bibliography on The Middle East Crisis

Prepared by Anthony P. Grech

*Librarian, The Association of the Bar of the City of New York*

## GENERAL

Allon, Yigal. The Arab-Israel conflict—some suggested solutions. April 1964. 40 Int'l Aff. (London) 205-18.

American Zionist Council. Israel and the Arab states, the issues in dispute: Israel's frontiers and the Arab refugees. New York, American Zionist Council. 1951. 30p.

The Arab-Israel conflict: the establishment of Israel; the balance of power 1950-57. 17 External Aff. Rev. 3-15 (March 1967); 3-16 (June 1967).

Arab-Israel relations. Dec. 9, 1966. 12 Commonwealth Survey 1245-57.

Arnery, Uri. Israel without Zionists. A plea for peace in the middle east. New York, Macmillan. 1968. 215p.

Berger, Earl. The covenant and the sword: Arab-Israeli relations 1948-56. Toronto, Univ. of Toronto Press. 1965. 245p.

Bernstein, Marver H. The politics of Israel; the first decade of statehood. Princeton, Princeton Univ. Press. 1957. 360p.

Binder, Leonard. The middle east crisis: background and issues. Chicago, Univ. of Chicago, Center for Political Study. 1967. 27p.

Brook, D. Preface to peace; the United Nations and Arab-Israel armistice system. Washington, Public Affairs Press. 1964. 151p.

Le conflit israélo-arabe. 1966. 16 Rev. Française de Science Politique 753-98.

El-Farra, Muhammad H. The role of the United Nations vis-à-vis the Palestine question. 1968. 33 Law & Contemp. Prob. 68-77.

Ellis, Harry B. Israel and the middle east. New York, Ronald Press. 1957. 260p.

Elston, D. R.   Israel: the making of a nation. New York, Oxford Univ. Press. 1963. 159p.

The establishment of Israel.   1967. 17 (3) External Aff. Rev. 3-15.

Eytan, Walter.   The first ten years: a diplomatic history of Israel. New York, Simon & Schuster. 1958. 239p.

Forward, R. H., jr., et al. The Arab-Israeli war and international law. 1968. 9 Harv. Int'l L. J. 232-76.

Gervasi, Frank.   The case for Israel. New York, Viking. 1967. 258p.

Halderman, John W.   Some international constitutional aspects of the Palestine case. 1968. 33 Law & Contemp. Prob. 78-96.

Hamzeh, F. S.   International conciliation, with special reference to the work of the United Nations Conciliation Commission for Palestine. The Hague, Drukerij Pasmans. 1963. 177p.

Hashem, Zaki.   Some international law aspects of the Palestine question. 1967. 23 Rev. Egyptienne de Droit International 63-107.

Institute for Palestine Studies.   United Nations resolutions on Palestine 1947-1965. Beirut. 1965. 157p.

The international status of Palestine. 1963. 90 J. du Droit International 964-85.

Israel.   Ministry of Foreign Affairs.   Israel's peace offers to Arab states, 1948-58; The Record. Jerusalem, Gov't. Printer. 1958. 62p.

Israel.   Office of Information.   Israel's struggle for peace. New York 1960. 187p.

Jerusalem. Hebrew University. Israel and the United Nations. Report of a study group set up by the Hebrew University of Jerusalem. Prepared for the Carnegie endowment for international peace. New York, Manhattan Pub. Co. 1956. 322p.

Johnson, U. A. American policy in the near east. Feb. 10, 1964. 50 Dep't State Bull. 208-11.

Khouri, Fred J. The Arab-Israeli dilemma. Syracuse, Syracuse Univ. Press. 1968. 436p.

Lavergne, B. Le problème d'Israël. Oct. 1967. 40 Ann. Politique et Economique 210-26.

Leonard, L. L. The United Nations and Palestine. Oct. 1949. Int'l Conciliation 603-786.

O'Brien, W. V. International law and the outbreak of war in the middle east. 1967. 11 Orbis 692-724.

Peretz, Don. Israel and the Arab nations. 1965. 19 J. Int'l Aff. 100-10.

Polk, William R. The United States and the Arab world. Cambridge, Harvard Univ. Press. 1965. 320p.

Rodinson, M. Israel: the Arab options. 1968. 22 Yb. World Aff. 80-92.

Rosenne, Shabtai. Israël et traités internationaux de la Palestine. 1950. 77 J. du Droit International 1140-73.

Safran, Nadav.
The Arab-Israeli dispute in perspective. 1967. 53 Current Hist. 321-30.

The United States and Israel. Cambridge, Harvard Univ. Press. 1963. 341p.

Studi, M. The Palestine case: a challenge to human conscience. 1968. 22 Int'l Spectator.

Tornetta, V. La questione palestinese e le Nazioni Unite. 1960. 27 Riv. di Studi Politici Internazionali 51-121.

U.S. Congress. Senate. Comm. on Foreign Relations.
(90.1) Hearings, arms sales to near East and south Asian countries. Washington, Gov't Print. Off. 1967. 120p.

(90.1) A select chronology and background documents relating to the middle East. June 6, 1967. Washington, Gov't Print. Off. 1967. 151p.

U.S. Department of State. Office of the Geographer. International boundary study. Israel-United Arab Republic armistice line. Washington. 1965. 7p.

Wilner, I. Toward a new solution of the Arab-Israel controversy. 1963/64. 126 World Aff. 244-49.

Wright, Quincy. Legal aspects of the middle east situation. 1968. 33 Law & Contemp. Prob. 5-31.

## HISTORICAL BACKGROUND PRIOR TO U.N. PARTITION PLAN

Abcarius, Michel Fred. Palestine through the fog of propaganda. London, Hutchinson. 1946. 240p.

Akzin, Benjamin. The Palestine mandate in practice. 1939. 25 Iowa L. Rev. 32-77.

Andrews, Fannie Fern (Phillips). The Holy land under mandate. Boston, Houghton Mifflin. 1931. 2v.

Anglo-American Committee of Inquiry on Jewish Problems in Palestine and Europe. Report to the United States government and His Majesty's government in the United Kingdom, Lausanne, Switzerland, 20 April 1946. Washington, Gov't Print. Off. 1946. 92p.

Ashkenazi, Touvia and Locker, Chaim, comps. Palestine: treaties, agreements and pronouncements. Pittsburgh, Kedem. 1947. 241p.

Balfour, Arthur James, earl of. Speeches on Zionism. London, Arrowsmith. 1928. 128p.

Barbour, Nevill. Palestine: star or crescent? New York, Odyssey Press. 1947. 310p.

Baumkoller, Abraham. Le mandat sur la Palestine. Paris, Rousseau. 1931. 354p.

Baumont, M. Origines historiques de l'état d'Israël. June 15, 1967. Rev. des Deux Mondes 486-99.

Bentwich, Norman De Mattos.
England in Palestine. London, Kegan Paul. 1932. 358p.

Israel resurgent. New York, Praeger. 1960. 255p.

Judicial interpretation of the mandate for Palestine. 1929. Band I, Teil I Zeitschrift für Ausländisches Offentliches Recht und Völkerrecht 212-22.

Palestine. London, Benn. 1934. 302p.

Palestine and the Jews. London, Kegan Paul. 1919. 288p.

Le système des mandats (in Hague. Academy of international law. Recueil des cours, 1929, IV (v.29, pp. 115-86).

Bississo, Saadi. La politique anglo-sioniste en Palestine. Paris, Rodstein. 1937. 278p.

Boustany, Wedi'Faris. The Palestine mandate invalid and impracticable; a contribution of arguments and documents towards the solution of the Palestine problem. Beirut, Printed at the American Press. 1936. 168p.

Cohn, Josef. England und Palästina. Berlin, Vowinckel. 1931. 327p.

Crossman, Richard H. S.
The Balfour declaration 1917-1967. Dec. 1967. 13 Midstream 21-28.

Palestine mission: a personal record. New York, Harper. 1947. 210p.

Cunningham, A. Palestine—the last days of the mandate. Oct. 1948. 24 Int'l Aff. 481-90.

De Haas, Jacob. History of Palestine: the last two thousand years. New York, Macmillan. 1934. 550p.

Esco Foundation for Palestine, Inc. Palestine, a study of Jewish, Arab and British policies. New Haven, Yale Univ. Press. 1947. 2v.

Feinberg, Nathan. Some problems of the Palestine mandate. Tel-Aviv, Shoshani's Printing Co. 1936. 125p.

Fischer, Heinz C. La colonisation juive en Palestine. Paris, Lipschutz. 1937. 173p.

Frankenstein, Ernst. Palestine in the light of international law. London, Narod Press. 1946. 54p.

Frischwasser-Ra'anan, Heinz Felix. The frontiers of a nation. London, Batchworth. 1955. 168p.

Gelber, M. Hazharat Balfour utoldoteah. Jerusalem, Zionist Executive. 1939. 360p.

Gellner, Charles Raymond. The Palestine problem, an analysis, historical and contemporary. Washington. 1947. 188p. (U.S. Library of Congress, Legislative reference service, Pub. Aff. bull. no. 50).

Great Britain. Colonial Office. Various reports on Palestine from 1922 to 1938.

Great Britain: Commission on Palestine Disturbances of August 1929.

Evidence heard during the 1st-47th sittings. London. 1930. 3v. (Colonial no. 48).

Report of the Commission on the Palestine disturbances of August 1929. London, H. M. Stat. Off. 1930. 202p.

Great Britain. Parliament. Final drafts of the mandates for Mesopotamia and Palestine for the approval of the council of the League of Nations presented to Parliament, Aug. 1921. 13p.

Hadawi, Sami. Bitter harvest: Palestine between 1914-1967. New York, New World Press. 1967. 355p.

Hanna, Paul L. British policy in Palestine. Washington, American Council on Public Affairs. 1942. 214p.

Horowitz, David. State in the making. New York, Knopf. 1953. 349p.

Howard, Harry N. The King-Crane commission: an American inquiry in the middle east. Beirut, Khayats. 1963. 369p.

Hurewitz, Jacob C. The struggle for Palestine. New York, Norton. 1950. 404p.

Hyamson, Albert M. Palestine under the mandate, 1920-1948. London, Methuen. 1950. 210p.

Jannaway, Frank George. Palestine and the world. London, Sampson Low. 1922. 268p.

Jeffries, J. M. N. Palestine: the reality. London, Longmans, Green. 1939. 728p.

Johnsen, Julia Emily, comp. Palestine: Jewish homeland? New York, H. W. Wilson. 1946. 342p.

Joseph, Bernard. British rule in Palestine. Washington, Public Affairs Press. 1948. 279p.

Linowitz, Sol M. Analysis of a tinderbox: the legal basis for the state of Israel: beginning with the Balfour declaration of 1917 and concluding with the establishment of the State of Israel by the United Nations in 1947. 1957. 43 A. B. A. J. 522-25.

Marlowe, John, pseud.
Rebellion in Palestine. New York, Heinman. 1946. 279p.

The seat of Pilate: an account of the Palestine mandate. London, Cresset. 1959. 289p.

Moch, Maurice. Le mandat britannique en Palestine. Paris, A. Mechelinck. 1932. 416p.

Nutting, A. The tragedy of Palestine from the Balfour declaration to today. Spring 1968. Issues 1-10.

Palestine. Memoranda prepared by the government of Palestine. London, H. M. Stat. Off. 1937. 207p. (Gt. Brit. Colonial office, Colonial no. 33).

Palestine Arab Refugee Office, New York. Official documents, pledges and resolutions on Palestine, beginning with the Husain-McMahon correspondence 1916; documents of special interest in any study of the Palestine case. New York. 1959. 161p.

Parkes, James W. A history of Palestine from 135 A. D. to modern times. New York, Oxford Univ. Press. 1949. 391p.

Pic, P. Le régime du mandat d'après le traité de Versailles; son application dans le proche orient. Mandats français en Syrie, anglais en Palestine et Mésopotamie. 1923. 30 Rev. Générale de Droit International Public 321-71.

Polk, William Roe; Stamber, David M. and Asfour, Edmund. Backdrop to tragedy: the struggle for Palestine. Boston, Beacon Press. 1957. 399p.

Robinson, Jacob. Palestine and the United Nations; prelude to solution. Washington, Public Affairs Press. 1947. 269p.

Sakran, Frank C. Palestine dilemma. Washington, Public Affairs Press. 1948. 230p.

Sharef, Zeev. Three days. Garden City, N.Y., Doubleday. 1962. 298p.

Stein, Leonard Jacques. The Balfour declaration. New York, Simon & Schuster. 1961. 681p.

Stoyanovsky, J. The mandate for Palestine. New York, Longmans. 1928. 414p.

Sykes, Christopher. Crossroads to Israel. London, Collins. 1965. 479p.

Tuchman, Barbara. Bible and sword: England and Palestine from the bronze age to Balfour. New York, New York Univ. Press. 1956. 268p.

U.S. Congress. House. Comm. on Foreign Affairs. (67.2) Establishment of a national home in Palestine. Hearings . . . on H. Con. Res. 52 expressing satisfaction at the re-creation of Palestine as the national home of the Jewish race, April 18-21, 1922. Washington, Gov't Print. Off. 1922. 170p.

Weisman, Herman L. The future of Palestine; an examination of the partition plan. New York. 1937. 138p.

Wise, Stephen S. and De Haas, Jacob. The great betrayal. New York, Brentano. 1930. 315p.

Wright, Quincy. Mandates under the League of Nations. Chicago, Univ. of Chicago Press. 1930. 726p.

Wright, Quincy. The Palestine problem. 1926. 41 Pol. Sci. Q. 384-412.

Ziff, William Bernard. The rape of Palestine. New York, Longmans. 1938. 612p.

## U.N. PARTITION PLAN

Bernadotte of Wisborg, Folke, greve. To Jerusalem. London, Hodder. 1951. 280p.

Elaraby, Nabil. Some legal implications of the 1947 partition resolution and the 1949 armistice agreements. 1968. 33 Law & Contemp. Prob. 97-109.

Great Britain. Colonial Office. Palestine; termination of the mandate 15 May 1948. Statement prepared for public information by the Colonial office and foreign office. London, H. M. Stat. Off. 1948. 11p.

Hadawi, Sami, ed. Palestine partitioned, 1947-1958. New York, Arab Information Center. 1959. 42p.

Israel. Ministry of Foreign Aairs. What happened to the 1947 U.N. resolution. Jerusalem. 15p. 1960.

Israel. Ministry of Foreign Affairs. U.N. resolutions—the Arab record. Jerusalem, Information Division. 1960. 7p.

Israel. Mission to the United Nations. Israel before the Security council, May 15-July 15, 1948; a record of fidelity to the United Nations. New York. 1948. 67p.

Palestine Arab Refugees Institution. Resolutions adopted by the different organs of the U.N. on the Palestine question, 1947-1953. Damascus. 1953. 2d ed. 154p.

Palestine Arab Refugee Office, New York. United Nations resolutions on Palestine 1947-1961. Edited by Izzat Tannous. New York. 1961? 100p.

Leonard, Leonard Larry. The United Nations and Palestine. Oct. 1949. 454 Int'l Conciliation 603-786.

United Nations. Conciliation Commission for Palestine.
General progress report dated 2 Sept. 1950 to the Secretary-general of the United Nations. Lake Success. 1950. 70p.

Progress report 1st—24 Jan. 1949—. Lake Success.

United Nations. General Assembly. Special Comm. on Palestine. Report to the second session of the general assembly. Lake Success. 1947. 5v.

United Nations. Mediator on Palestine.
Progress report submitted to the Secretary-general for transmission to the members of the United Nations in pursuance of par. 2, pt. II of resolution 186 (S-2) of the general assembly, 14 May 1948. Paris. 1948. 57p.

Report dated 16 Sept. 1948 on the observation of the truce in Palestine during the period from 11 June to 9 July 1948. Lake Success. 1948. 38p.

United Nations. Palestine Commission. Report to the second special session of the general assembly. Lake Success. 1948. 39p.

Welles, Sumner. We need not fail. Boston, Houghton Mifflin. 1948. 143p.

## MILITARY ACTION OF 1948

Bilby, Kenneth W. New star in the near east. Garden City, N.Y., Doubleday. 1950. 279p.

Joseph, Dov. The faithful city; the siege of Jerusalem 1948. New York, Simon & Schuster. 1960. 357p.

Kimche, Jon and Kimche, David. A clash of destinies; the Arab-Jewish war and the founding of the state of Israel. New York, Praeger. 1960. 287p.

Lorch, Netanel. The edge of the sword: Israel's war of independence, 1947-1949. New York, Putnam. 1961. 475p.

Rosenne, Shabtai. Israel's armistice agreements with the Arab states; a juridical interpretation. Tel Aviv, Published for the International Law Association, Israel Branch by Blumstein's Bookstores. 1951. 98p.

Texte des conventions d'armistice conclués entre le gouvernement d'Israël et les gouvernements égyptien, jordanais, libanais et syrien. Dec. 1, 1949. 1238 Documentation Française. Notes et Etudes Documentaires 1-22.

## MILITARY ACTION OF 1956

Adams, Michael. Suez and after: year of crisis. Boston, Beacon Press. 1958. 225p.

Aldrich, W. W. The Suez crisis: a footnote. 1967. 45 For. Aff. 541-52.

Aroneanu, E. Le conflict israélo-égyptien et la justice internationale. Jan/March 1957. 35 Rev. de Droit International de Sciences Diplomatiques et Politiques 5-14.

Barker, A. J. Suez: the seven day war. New York, Praeger. 1965. 223p.

Bartos, M. L'aspect juridique de l'agression en Egypte. Nov. 16, 1956. 7 Rev. de la Politique Internationale 3-5.

Blechman, B. M. The quantitative evaluation of foreign policy alternatives: Sinai 1965. 1966. 10 J. Conflict Resolution 408-26.

Briggs, E. D. Crisis and world opinion: Suez in retrospect. Winter 1967. 74 Queens Q. 610-26.

Canada. Department of External Affairs. The crisis in the middle east, October/December 1956-January/March 1957 by Hon. Lester B. Pearson, secretary of state for external affairs. Ottawa, E. Cloutier. 1957. 2v. in 1.

Childers, Erskine B. The road to Suez: a study of western-Arab relations. London, Macgibbon. 1962. 416p.

Dayan, Moshe. Diary of the Sinai campaign. New York, Harper & Row. 1966. 236p.

95

Eayrs, James George, ed. The Commonwealth and Suez; a documentary survey, selected, edited and with commentaries. New York, Oxford Univ. Press. 1964. 483p.

Epstein, Leon D. British politics in the Suez crisis. Urbana, Univ. of Illinois Press. 1964. 220p.

Henriques Quixano, Robert David. A hundred hours to Suez. New York, Viking. 1957. 206p.

The Israel-Egypt conflict. Nov. 15, 1956. 23 Vital Speeches of the Day 66-79.

Israel. Misrad rosh ha-menshalah.
International law or anarchy in the middle east; statement of policy by the Prime minister of Israel, Mr. David Ben-Gurion ...Jan. 23, 1957. Jerusalem, Ministry for Foreign Affairs. 1957. 14p.

Israel. Ministry of Foreign Affairs. Egyptian violations of international law. Jerusalem, Government Printer. 1957. 15p.

Israel. Office of Information. Nasser's pattern of aggression. Captured documents reveal army and fedayeen roles in Egyptian plot against peace. New York, Israel Office of Information. 1957. 32p.

Johnson, Paul. The Suez war...Foreword by Aneurin Bevan. London, Macgibbon, Kee. 1957. 145p.

Marshall, Samuel L. A. Sinai victory: command decisions in history's shortest war. New York. 1958. 280p.

Moncrieff, Anthony, ed. Suez: ten years after. Intro. by Peter Calvocoressi. New York, Pantheon Books. 1967. 160p.

Nutting, Anthony. No end of a lesson: the story of Suez. New York, Potter. 1967. 205p.

O'Ballance, Edgar. The Sinai campaign of 1956. New York, Praeger. 1960. 223p.

Robertson, Terence. Crisis: the inside story of the Suez conspiracy. New York, Atheneum. 1965. 349p.

Smolansky, O. M. Moscow and the Suez crisis 1956—a reappraisal. 1965. 80 Pol. Sci. Q. 581-605.

Stock, Ernest. Israel on the road to Sinai 1949-56; with a sequel on the six day war. Ithaca, Cornell Univ. Press. 1967. 284p.

Watt, Donald Cameron, ed. Documents on the Suez crisis, 26 July to 6 November 1956. New York, Oxford Univ. Press (for the Royal Institute of International Affairs). 1957. 88p.

Wint, Guy and Calvocoressi, Peter. Middle east crisis. Baltimore, Penguin. 1957. 141p.

## LEGAL RIGHTS OF ARAB REFUGEES

Akriche, R. Le problème des réfugiés et le conflit israélo-arabe—propositions pour la paix. Sept. 1966. 34 Esprit 273-305.

Avnery, U. The Arab refugees. Aug. 8, 1959. 11 Econ. Weekly 1111-16.

Dimitrijević, V. Le statut juridique des réfugiés palestiniens. Jan. 20, 1968. 19 Rev. de la Politique Internationale (Belgrade) 17-18.

Dodge, B. The problem of the Palestine refugees. Sept. 1949. 39 Yale Rev. 61-74.

Erim, T. K. Le "réfugié" de la Palestine. May 1953. 2 Rev. de Droit International pour le Moyen-Orient 116-24.

Gabbay, Romy E. A political study of the Arab-Jewish conflict: the Arab refugee problem. Geneva, Droz. 1959. 611p.

Grahl-Madwen, Athe. The status of refugees in international law. Leyden, Sijthoff. 1966. 499p.

Holborn, L. W. The Palestine Arab refugee problem. Winter 1967-1968. 23 Int'l J. 82-96.

Hottinger, A. The Palestinian refugees—an unsolved problem. Nov. 1961. 11 Swiss Rev. World Aff. 4-8.

Howard, H. N. UNRWA's technical assistance program among Arab refugees. April/June 1964. 127 World Aff. 23-28.

Krenz, Frank E. The refugee as a subject of international law. 1966. 15 Int'l & Comp. L. Q. 90-116.

Lalive, J. F. Le statut juridique de l'Office de secours et de travaux des Nations Unies pour les réfugiés de Palestine. Nov. 1954. 3 Rev. de Droit International pour le Moyen-Orient 304-21.

Ludlow, J. M. The Arab refugees—a decade of dilemma for the United Nations. Nov. 17, 1958. 38 Dept' State Bull. 775-81.

Mac Innes, A. C. The Arab refugee problem. 1949. 36 Royal Central Asian J. 178-88.

Mezerik, A. G., ed. Arab refugees in the middle east. New York, International Review Service. 1958. 70p.

Palestine refugee aid. Jan. 1959. 5 U.N. Rev. 42-45.

The Palestine refugees. June 1962. 33 Current Notes on Int'l Aff. (Australia) 17-24.

The Palestine refugee problem: a new approach and a plan for a solution. New York, Institute for Mediterranean Affairs. 1958. 133p.

The Palestine refugee program. May 1957. 3 U.N. Rev. 30-37, 67-69.

Paulnet, M. Le problème des réfugiés arabes de Palestine. June 1960. 7 Monde Diplomatique 7-10.

Peretz, Don.
The Arab-Israeli war; Israel's administration and Arab refugees. 1968. 46 For. Aff. 336-46.

The Arab refugee dilemma. Oct. 1954. 33 For Aff. 134-48.

The Arab refugees: a changing problem. 1963. 41 For. Aff. 558-70.

Israel and the Palestine Arabs. Washington, Middle East Institute. 1958. 264p.

Problems of Arab refugee compensation. Autumn 1954. 8 Middle East J. 403-16.

Schechtman, Joseph B.
The Arab refugee problem. New York, Philosophical Library. 1952. 137p.

Arab refugee problem reassessed. March 18, 1963. 30 Congress Bi-weekly 11-13.

A census of Arab refugees. Feb. 2, 1959. 26 Congress Bi-weekly 5-7.

Thabit, R. W. History and summary of United Nations aid to Arab refugees. Dec. 1952. 5 Bull. Near East Soc'y 10-11.

Thicknesse, S. G. Arab refugees, a survey of resettlement possibilities. London, New York, Royal Institute of International Affairs. 1949. 68p.

Tomeh, George J. Legal status of Arab refugees. 1968. 33 Law & Contemp. Prob. 110-24.

United Arab Republic. The problem of the Palestinian refugees. Cairo. 1964. 98p.

U.S. Congress. House. Comm. on Foreign Affairs.
(81.2) Palestine refugees. Hearings . . . on S. J. Res. 153. Washington, Gov't Print. Off. 1950. 76p.

(83.2) The Arab refugees and other problems in the near east. Report of the Special study mission to the near east . . . Lawrence H. Smith, chairman. Washington, Gov't Print. Off. 1954. 23p.

U.S. Congress. Senate. Comm. on Foreign Relations.
  (83.1) Palestine refugee program. Hearings before the subcom. on the near east and Africa... May 20-25, 1953. Washington, Gov't Print. Off. 1953. 120p.

  Palestine refugee program; background information for study of the Palestine refugee program. Staff memorandum for subcom. on near east and Asia. Washington, Gov't Print. Off. 1953. 26p.

  Palestine refugee problem. Report of the subcom. on the near east and Africa... on the problem of Arab refugees from Palestine. Washington, Gov't Print. Off. 1953. 4p.

U.S. Department of State. Working Group on Legislation for the Arab Refugee Program. The Palestine refugee program. Washington. 1950. 39p.

Zarhi, S. Economics of refugee settlement. New outlook. Dec. 1967. 10 Middle East Monthly 31-35.

## INTERNATIONAL AND LEGAL STATUS
## OF THE SUEZ CANAL

Aguilar Navarro, M. El canal de Suez y el problema del control internacional. Oct. 1957. 33 Política Internacional 47-111.

American Society of Intednational Law. International law and the middle east crisis; a symposium of papers originally delivered at the regional meeting of the American society of international law, April 6, 1957, Tulane university. New Orleans, Tulane Univ. Press. 1957. 93p.

Aspects du probléme du canal de Suez. 1957. 13 Rev. Egyptienne de Droit International 99-110.

Avran, Benno. The evolution of the Suez canal status from 1869 up to 1956; a historico-juridical study. Genève, Droz. 1958. 170p.

Babović, Bogdan. The international legal position of the Suez canal and nationalization. 1960. Int'l Prob. (Belgrade) 191-216.

Badawi, Abdel Hamid. Le statut international du canal de Suez (in Mélanges Speropoulos. Bonn, Schimmelbusch, 1957, pp. 13-36).

Badeau, J. S. The significance of the Suez canal in current international affairs. 1954. 20 Vital Speeches of the Day 200-5.

Baxter, Richard R.
  The law of international waterways, with particular regard to interoceanic canals. Cambridge, Harvard Univ. Press. 1964. 371p.

Passage of ships through international waterways in time of war. 1954. 31 Brit. Yb. Int'l L. 187-216.

Bisegna, A. La questione di Suez. 1967. 11 Stato Sociale 577-607.

Boutros-Ghali, B. et Chlala, Youssef. Le canal de Suez (1854-1957). Alexandrie, Société Egyptien Droit International. 1958. 211p.

Buiskool, Johannes A. E. De internationalisatie van het Suez-kanaal. Zwolle, Willink. 1938. 28p.

British Institute of International and Comparative Law. The Suez canal. A selection of documents relating to the international status of the Suez canal and the position of the Suez canal company, Nov. 30, 1854-July 25, 1956. London, Society of Comparative Legislation and International Law. 1956. 76p.

British Institute of International and Comparative Law. The Suez canal settlements; a selection of documents relating to the settlement of the Suez canal dispute, the clearance of the Suez canal and the settlement of disputes between the United Kingdom, France and the United Arab Republic, Oct. 1956-March 1959. Edited by E. Lauterpacht. London, Stevens; New York, Praeger. 1960. 82p.

Castaneda, J. Certain legal consequences of the Suez crisis. 1963. 19 Rev. Égyptienne de Droit International 1-15.

Castella, Pedro. La crisis del canal de Suez; antecedentes político-Jurídicos en el texto de la convención de 1888. Buenos Aires, Ediciones Theoría. 1956. 64p.

Compagnie Universelle du Canal Maritime de Suez. The Suez canal company and the decision taken by the Egyptian government on 26 July 1956. Paris, Imprimerie S. E. F. 1956-57. 2v.

Compagnie Universelle du Canal Maritime de Suez. Recueil chronologique des actes constitutifs de la Compagnie universelle du canal maritime de Suez et des conventions conclués avec le gouvernement égyptien, 30 novembre 1854-1 janvier 1950. Paris, Imprimerie Desfosses. 1950. 370p.

Conference on the Suez Canal, London, 1956. The Suez canal conference; selected documents, London, Aug. 2-24, 1956. London, H. M. Stat. Off. 1956. 18p. (Papers by command, cmd 9853).

Dehaussy, J. La déclaration égyptienne de 1957 sur le canal de Suez. 1960. 6 Ann. Française de Droit International 169-84.

Delson, Robert. Nationalization of the Suez canal company: issues of public and private international law. 1957. 57 Colum. L. Rev. 755-86.

Dinitz, Simcha. The legal aspects of the Egyptian blockade of the Suez canal. 1956/57. 45 Geo. L. J. 169-99.

Eayrs, James, ed. The Commonwealth and Suez: a documentary survey. New York, Oxford Univ. Press. 1964. 483p.

Egypt. Ministry of Foreign Affairs. White paper on the nationalisation of the Suez maritime canal company. Cairo, Government Press. 1956. 72p.

Generales, Minos D. Suez: national sovereignty and international waterways. 1958. 29 World Aff. 177-90.

Ghobashy, Omar Z.
     The Egyptian Israeli dispute on the freedom of navigation in the Suez canal. 1955. 11 Rev. Egyptienne de Droit International 121-31.

     Israel and Suez canal. April 1960. 6 Egyptian Econ. & Pol. Rev. 9-13.

Gross, Leo. Passage through the Suez canal of Israel-bound cargo and Israel ships. 1957. 51 Am. J. Int'l L. 530-68.

Hostie, Jan. F. Notes on the international statute of the Suez canal. 1957. 31 Tulane L. Rev. 397-436.

International control of the Suez canal (a symposium). 1967. 2 Int'l Law. 27-50.

Israel. Ministry of Foreign Affairs. Egypt and the Suez canal 1948-1959; a record of lawlessness. Jerusalem, Ministry for Foreign Affairs, Information Division. 1959. 11p.

Khadduri, Majid. Closure of the Suez canal to Israeli shipping. 1968. 3 Law & Contemp. Prob. 147-57.

Khatib, M. F. and Ghobashy, O. Z. The Suez canal: safe and free passage. New York, Arab Information Center. 1960. 47p.

Lauterpacht, E., ed. The Suez canal settlement. New York, Praeger (for the British Institute of International and Comparative Law). 1960. 82p.

The law of international waterways: an approach to a Suez canal solution. 1957. 105 U. Pa. L. Rev. 714-44.

Lawyers Committee on Blockades. The United Nations and the Egyptian blockade of the Suez canal. New York. 1953. 26p.

Lee, Luke T. Legal aspects of internationalization of interoceanic canals. 1968. 33 Law & Contemp. Prob. 158-68.

101

Mensbrugghe, Y. V. D. Les garanties de la liberté navigation dans le canal de Suez. Paris, Pichon et Durand-Auzias. 1964. 430p.

Obieta, Joseph A. The international status of the Suez canal. The Hague, Nijhoff. 1960. 137p.

Rauschning, Dietrich.
Der streit um Suezkanal. Hamburg, Forschungsstelle für Völkerrecht und Ausländisches Offentliches Recht. 1956. 187p.

Rechtsprobleme der Suezkanal-krise. 1956. 7 Jahrbuch für Internationales Recht 257-82.

Schonfield, Hugh Joseph. The Suez canal in world affairs. New York, Philosophical Library. 1953. 174p.

Stillman, A. M. The United Nations and the Suez canal. Ann Arbor, University Microfilms. 1965. 238p.

Thomas, Hugh. The Suez affair. New York, Harper & Row. 1967. 261p.

United Arab Republic. Maslahat al-Ist'lāmāt.Navigation in the Suez canal—Israeli pretensions refuted by documents. Cairo, Information Department, U.A.R. 1961. 45p.

U.S. Department of State. Library Division. The Suez crisis; a chronological list. Washington. 1956. 15p.

Visscher, Paul de. Les aspects juridiques fondamentaux de la question de Suez. 1958. 62 Rev. Générale de Droit International Public 400-43.

Watt, Donald Cameron. Documents on the Suez crisis, 26 July to 6 November 1956. Selected and introduced by D. C. Watt. London, Royal Institute of International Affairs. 1957. 88p.

Huang, Thomas T. F. Some international and legal aspects of the Suez canal question. 1957. 51 Am. J. Int'l L. 277-307.

## INTERNATIONAL AND LEGAL STATUS OF THE GULF OF AQABA AND STRAITS OF TIRAN

The Aqaba question and international law. 1957. 13 Rev. Egyptienne de Droit International 86-94.

Bloomfield, Louis Mortimer. Egypt, Israel and the gulf of Aqaba in international law. Toronto, Carswell. 1957. 240p.

Bruel, Erik. International straits, a treatise on international law. London, Sweet & Maxwell. 1947. 2v.

Cagle, Malcolm W. The gulf of Aqaba—trigger for conflict. Jan. 1959. 85 U.S. Naval Inst. Proc. 75-81.

Geniewski, P. (L')Egypte a-t-elle le droit de contrôler le golfe d'Akaba? 1955. Politique Étrangère 595-602.

Ghobashy, Omar Z. Tiran and Aqaba. Jan. 1959. 5 Egyptian Econ. Pol. Rev. (2d ser) 18-25.

Gross, Leo.
   The Geneva conference on the law of the sea and the right of innocent passage through the gulf of Aqaba. 1959. 53 Am. J. Int'l L. 564-94.

   Passage through the strait of Tiran and in the gulf of Aqaba. 1968. 33 Law & Contemp. Prob. 125-46.

The gulf of Aqaba and the Suez canal convention. 1957. 13 Rev. Egyptienne de Droit International 111-13.

Hammad, M. Burhan. The right of passage in the gulf of Aqaba. 1959. 15 Rev. Egyptienne de Droit International 118-51.

Hartwig, B. Der israelisch-agyptische streit um den golf von Akaba. 1961. 9 Archiv des Völkerrechts 27-46.

Israel. Ministry of Foreign Affairs. Background paper on the gulf of Aqaba. Jerusalem. 1956. 16p.

Israel. Office of Information. The gulf of Akaba. Free navigation or return to piracy. New York, Israel Office of Information. 1957. 8p.

Lowe, G. The crisis in western Asia—the Arab-Israeli war underlines the need for international agreements quaranteeing freedom of the seas and access to waterways. Oct. 1967. 1 Interplay of European & Am. Aff. 36-40.

Melamid, Alexander. Legal status of the gulf of Aqaba. 1959. 53 Am. J. Int'l L. 412-13.

Murti, B.S.N. The legal status of the gulf of Aqaba. 1967. 7 Ind. J. Int'l L. 201-6.

Porter, Paul A. The gulf of Aqaba: an international waterway. Its significance to international trade. Washington, Public Affairs Press. 1957. 18p.

Rabbath, Edmond. Mer rouge et golfe d'Aqaba dans l'évolution du droit international. Le Caire. 1962. 52p. (Société égyptienne de droit international, brochure no. 16).

Selak, Charles B., Jr. A consideration of the legal status of the gulf of Aqaba. 1958. 52 Am. J. Int'l L. 660-98.

Speyer, J. M. The gulf of Aqaba; a political problem of juridical status. 1957. 11 Int'l Spectator 315-37.

Strohl, Mitchell P. The international law of bays. The Hague, Nijhoff. 1963. 426p.

## ARAB-ISRAELI BORDER PROBLEMS

Alexander, L. M. The Arab-Israeli boundary problem. April 1954. 6 World Politics 322-37.

Bar-Yaacov, N. The Israel-Syrian armistice: problems of implementation, 1949-1966. Jerusalem, Magnes Press of Hebrew University. 1967. 377p.

Bentwich, Norman De Mattos. The Israel-Syrian armistice agreement. Oct. 1967. 3 Int'l Relations 253-58.

Burns, Eedson Louis Millard. Between Arab and Israeli. London, Harrap. 1962. 336p.

Dayan, Moshe. Israel's border and security problem. Jan. 1955. 33 For. Aff. 250-67.

Franck, Thomas M. and Gold, Kenneth H. The limits of perceptual objectivity in international peace observation. 1968. 33 Law & Contemp. Prob. 183-93.

Glubb, J. B. Violence on the Jordan-Israel border. 1953/54. 32 For. Aff. 552-62.

Howard, M. et Hunter, R. Les Nations Unies et la force d'urgence dans la crise israélo-arabe. 1967. 32 Politique Etrangère 397-405.

Hutchinson, Elmo H. Violent truce. New York, Devin-Adair. 1956. 199p.

Ionides, M. G. The disputed waters of Jordan. Spring 1953. 7 Middle East J. 153-64.

Khouri, Fred J.
Friction and conflict on the Israeli-Syrian front. Winter/Spring 1963. 17 Middle East J. 14-34.

The policy of retaliation in Arab-Israeli relations. 1966. 20 Middle East J. 435-55.

Rondot, P. Le raid de Samou et le conflit arabo-israélien. Jan. 1967. 23 Rev. de Défense 68-78.

Saliba, S. M. The Jordan river dispute. Ann Arbor, University Microfilms. 1966. 244p.

Schiff, Z. The dispute on the Syrian-Israeli border, new outlook. Feb. 1967. 10 Middle East Monthly 6-16.

Schmidt, D. A. Prospects for a solution of the Jordan river valley dispute. Jan. 1955. 6 Middle East Aff. 1-12.

Shwadran, B. Israel-Jordan border tension. Dec. 1953. 4 Middle East Aff. 385-401.

Soviet Union vetoes U.S.-U.K. resolution in Security council on Israel and Syrian complaints. Sept. 30, 1963. 49 U.S. Dep't State Bull. 520-23.

United Nations. Report dated 16 Feb. 1960 by the chief of staff of the United Nations truce supervision organization in Palestine to the Secretary-general concerning the recent incidents in the southern sector of the demilitarized zone created by art. V, par. 5 of the Israel-Syrian general armistice agreement. 1960. 15 U.N. Security Council Official Rec. (Supp. for Jan., Feb., March) 11-49.

U.S.S.R. vetoes Security council resolution on Israel complaint. Dec. 26, 1966. 55 Dep't State Bull. 969-78.

## MILITARY ACTION OF 1967

Bucher, H. H. et al. A symposium: the significance of the June 1967 Israeli-Arab war. Spring 1968. Issues 11-31.

Churchill, Randolph S. and Churchill, Winston S. The six day war. Boston, Houghton Mifflin. 1967. 250p.

Douglas-Home, Charles. The Arabs and Israel. Chester Springs, Pa., Dufour Editions. 1968.

Draper, Theodore. Israel and world politics: roots of the third Arab-Israeli war. New York, Viking. 1968. 278p.

Forward, Robert H., Jr. and others. The Arab-Israeli war and international law. 1968. 9 Harv. Int'l L. J. 232-76.

Howard, M. and Hunter, R. Israel and the Arab world: the crisis of 1967 (Adelphi Papers, no. 41, Oct. 1967).

Kimche, David and Bawly, Dan. The sandstorm: the Arab-Israeli war of June 1967: prelude and aftermath. New York, Stein & Day. 1968. 319p.

Laqueur, Walter. The road to Jerusalem: the origins of the Arab Israeli conflict. New York, Macmillan. 1968. 368p.

Lewis, Bernard. The Arab-Israeli war; the consequences of defeat. 1968. 46 For. Aff. 321-35.

105

Mac Leish, Roderick. The sun stood still. New York, Atheneum. 1967. 174p.

Mushhat, M. The recent middle-East conflict—some legal and socio-political issues. Feb. 22, 1968. 22 Int'l Spectator 258-78.

O'Brien, William V. International law and the outbreak of war in the middle east. 1967. Fall. 1967. 11 Orbis 692-723.

Rostow, Eugene V. The middle east crisis and beyond. Jan. 8, 1968. 58 Dep't State Bull. 41-48.

Rouleau, Eric et al. Israël et les arabes: le 3e combat. Paris, Editions du Seiul. 1967. 187p.

U Thant. The withdrawal of UNEF (United emergency force). Report. July 1967. 4 U.N. Monthly Chronicle 135-70.

Withdrawal of United Nations emergency force—some questions answered. June 1967. 4 U.N. Monthly Chronicle 87-94.

Yost, Charles W. The Arab-Israeli war; how it began. 1968. 46 For. Aff. 304-20.

Zavala, J. de. Algunos aspectos de interés militar de la crisis de oriente medio, 1967. July/Aug. 1967. Revista International 7-31.

## STATUS OF JERUSALEM

Berman, S. M. Territorial acquisition by conquest in international law and the unification of Jerusalem. May 1968. 7 Int'l Prob. 11-22.

Fitzgerald, W. An international régime for Jerusalem. 1950. 37 Royal Central Asian J. 273-83.

Garreau, Roger. Le statut international de Jérusalem. May 1955. Le Monde Diplomatique 1-3.

González Barros, Luis. Jerusalén y el futuro; ensayo histórico-jurídico sobre la internacionalización. Madrid, Ediciones Cultura Hispánica. 1958. 422p.

Great Britain. Report of the commission appointed by His Majesty's government ... to determine the rights and claims ... in connection with the western or Wailing wall at Jerusalem, Dec. 1930. (Distributed as U.N. Docs. A/7057/Add 1 and S/8427/Add 1 (Feb. 23, 1968).

Israeli letter of July 10, 1967 to the U.N. Secretary-general concerning the status of Jerusalem. 1967. 6 Int'l Leg. Materials 846-50.

Israel. Office of Information. Jerusalem and the United Nations. New York. 1953. 27p.

Jones, S. Shepard. The status of Jerusalem: some national and international aspects. 1968. 33 Law & Contemp. Prob. 169-82.

Katzarov, C. L'internationalisation de la ville de Jérusalem. 1950. 28 Rev. de Droit International des Sciences Diplomatiques et Politiques 400-10.

Las Cagigas, I. de. Sobre la internacionalización de Jerusalén. 1949. 2 Estudios Internacionales y Coloniales 65-75.

Mohn, Paul. Jerusalem and the United Nations. Oct. 1950. 464 Int'l Conciliation 421-71.

Le Nail, Pierre. Le probléme d' internationalisation de Jérusalem. Thése, Paris. 1954. 107p.

Peretz, Don. Jerusalem, a divided city. 1964. 18 J. Int'l Aff. 211-20.

Ruiz Moreno, I. El problema internacional de Jerusalén. (Lecciones y ensayos, Buenos Aires), 1965. 131-38.

Shertok, Moshe. The peace of Jerusalem; text of addresses presenting the position of the government of Israel on the future of Jerusalem during fourth session of the General assembly of the U.N., 1949, delivered by Moshe Sharett...and Aubrey S. Eban. New York, Israel Office of Information. 1949. 68p.

United Nations Security council resolution on Jerusalem 21 May 1968 (S/Res/252, 1968). 7 Int'l Leg. Materials 894.

## PEACE POSSIBILITIES

Peretz, Don. A binational approach to the Palestine conflict. 1968. 33 Law & Contemp. Prob. 32-43.

Rosenne, Shabtai. Directions for a middle east settlement—some underlying legal problems. 1968. 33 Law & Contemp. Prob. 44-67.

Shereshevsky, S. Peace without a peace treaty. July 1961. 4 Middle East Monthly 3-9.

U.N. Security council urges parties to settle middle east conflict. Oct. 14, 1968. 59 Dept' State Bull. 401-4.

Young, O.R. Intermediaries and interventionists: third parties in the middle east crisis. 1967/68. 23 Int'l J. 52-73.

*APPENDIX*

# TEXT OF THE UNITED NATIONS SECURITY COUNCIL RESOLUTION 242 ADOPTED BY THE SECURITY COUNCIL ON 22 NOVEMBER, 1967.

*The Security Council*

*Expressing* its continuing concern with the grave situation in the Middle East.

*Emphasizing* the inadmissibility of the acquisition of territory by war and the need to work for a just and lasting peace in which every State in the area can live in security.

*Emphasizing further* that all Member States in their acceptance of the Charter of the United Nations have undertaken a commitment to act in accordance with Article 2 of the Charter.

1. *Affirms* that the fulfilment of Charter principles requires the establishment of a just and lasting peace in the Middle East which should include the application of both the following principles:

 (i) Withdrawal of Israeli armed forces from territories occupied in the recent conflict;

 (ii) Termination of all claims or states of belligerency and respect for and acknowledgement of the sovereignty, territorial integrity and political independence of every State in the area and their right to live in peace within secure and recognized boundaries free from threats or acts of force;

2. *Affirms further* the necessity

 (a) For guaranteeing freedom of navigation through international waterways in the area;

 (b) For achieving a just settlement of the refugee problem;

 (c) For guaranteeing the territorial inviolability and political independence of every State in the area, through measures including the establishment of demilitarized zones;

3. *Requests* the Secretary-General to designate a Special Representative to proceed to the Middle East to establish and maintain contacts with the States concerned in order to promote agreement and assist efforts to achieve a peaceful and accepted settlement in accordance with the provisions and principles in this resolution;

4. *Requests* the Secretary-General to report to the Security Council on the progress of the efforts of the Special Representative as soon as possible.

# ARAB-ISRAELI DISPUTE—
# A CHRONOLOGY*

1897—A wave of anti-Semitism in Europe prompted a group of Jewish intellectuals meeting in Switzerland to promote the idea of a national homeland. The World Zionist Organization was formed.

1917—In return for international Jewish support for the Allied cause during World War I, Great Britain issued the Balfour Declaration favoring establishment in Palestine "of a national home for the Jewish people."

1919—The American King-Crane Commission concluded that the provisions of the Balfour Declaration could be implemented in Palestine only by the use of military force and at the expense of the non-Jewish population.

1922—Britain's allies (including the United States) approved the declaration, and it was incorporated into the League of Nations mandate for Palestine. Arabs reacted to the decision with periodic outbursts of violence.

1936—As Nazi persecution grew, so did the exodus of Jews to Palestine. By 1936, 25-30 percent of the population of Palestine were European Jews. Arab opposition grew more intense.

1937—A British Royal Commission declared the mandate to be unworkable. It recommended that Palestine be partitioned.

1939—Reacting to Arab pressure, Britain proposed giving up the mandate in favor of an independent predominantly Arab state to be established in 10 years. This proposal, in apparent contradiction of the Balfour Declaration and League mandate, inflamed Zionists; before the end of World War II Jewish immigrants began to organize to commit acts of terror and sabotage.

1944—U.S. Congress called for unlimited Jewish immigrants into Palestine and the reconstitution of Palestine as a Jewish commonwealth.

1947—Britain turned the Palestine problem over to the United Nations. Some members favored a federal state incorporating Arab and Jewish regions, but the majority—including the U.S. and U.S.S.R.—supported partition. In December, as British troops were withdrawing, civil war broke out between Arabs and Jews.

1948-49—Palestine Arab resistance collapsed; Israel proclaimed her independence May 14, 1948. At this point the conflict was taken up by the surrounding Arab states. By mid-year four Arab states had

---

* Reprinted from Department of State, Issues in United States Foreign Policy, No. 1 - The Middle East (1968).

agreed to an armistice. Israel occupied and continued to hold territory allotted to the Arab state, adding 50 percent to the territory originally allotted to the Jewish state. During this period most Israeli arms were supplied by Communist powers, notably Czechoslovakia, as well as clandestinely from private Western sources.

1953-56—Arab terrorists campaigned against Israel from Egypt and Jordan.

1955-56—Soviet arms deals with Egypt and Syria initiated a Soviet policy of extending large-scale military assistance to nationalist Arab regimes. Objecting to Egyptian nationalization of the Suez Canal Company and Egyptian aid to Algerian rebels, France and Britain in November 1956 joined Israel in attacking Egypt. Israel thereby opened the Strait of Tiran (which Egypt had refused to let Israel use since 1948, along with the Suez Canal), and terrorism against Israel from Egypt ended. Soviet and U.S. pressure brought the war to a quick end with a complete withdrawal of the attacking forces. Israel announced that any future Egyptian attempt to close the Strait of Tiran to Israel would be a *casus belli* (occasion for war).

1967—Terrorism against Israel from Syrian bases caused severe tension between Israel and Syria. The Soviets apparently provided a catalyst for the crisis by convincing the Syrian and Egyptian Governments that Israel was preparing to attack Syria. In May, United Arab Republic units moved in force into Sinai. Nasser demanded withdrawal of U.N. troops and the Secretary General immediately complied. On May 22, President Nasser closed the Strait of Tiran to Israeli shipping, bringing a protest from the U.S. and other maritime powers that this was a violation of the "right of innocent passage." President Nasser argued that Israel was still technically a "belligerent" and could not claim the right of innocent passage. On May 30, the U.A.R. and Jordan signed a mutual defense pact. Arab radio broadcasts spoke of exterminating Israel. On June 5, Israel, facing 80,000 U.A.R. troops in Sinai, 55,000 Jordanian troops, and 60,000 Syrian troops, took the offensive. Within 6 days Israel held the entire Sinai Peninsula, all Jordanian territory west of the Jordan including the strategic heights and city of Jerusalem, and a 12-mile bulge into Syria. The United Nations ordered a "cease-fire" on June 6. The Soviet Union started arms shipments to the Arab states immediately to replace equipment captured or destroyed by the Israeli Army. More than 200,000 new Palestinian Arab refugees were added to the million already living around the perimeter of Israel.

## DATE DUE

| | | | |
|---|---|---|---|
| APR 9 1987 | | | |
| MAR 14 1989 | | | |
| FEB 26 1991 | | | |
| | | | |
| | | | |
| | | | |
| | | | |
| | | | |
| | | | |
| | | | |
| | | | |
| | | | |
| | | | |
| | | | |
| | | | |
| | | | |